THE INTERNATIONAL SCHOOL OF
Sugarcraft

BOOK THREE • NEW SKILLS AND TECHNIQUES

THE INTERNATIONAL SCHOOL OF
Sugarcraft

BOOK THREE • NEW SKILLS AND TECHNIQUES

Principal teachers: Margaret Ford and Nicholas Lodge
Guest teachers: June Twelves, Marion Frost, Earlene Moore,
Toshie Harashima and Steven Stellingwerf

MEREHURST

Contents

In the USA, celebration cakes are mainly made using a heavy sponge, pound or madeira type of cake. Before the sugarpaste (rolled fondant) is added, the cakes are covered in a thin layer of buttercream. In the UK, fruit cakes are a popular choice. They are brushed with apricot glaze and covered with almond paste or marzipan. When dry, the almond paste is brushed with clear alcohol (gin or vodka), then sugarpaste or royal icing is used to cover the cake.

page 143

page 20

page 112

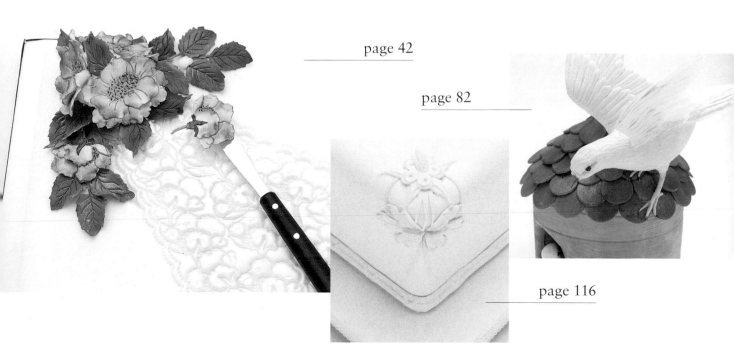

page 42

page 82

page 116

Introduction

Welcome to *The International School of Sugarcraft Book Three – New Skills and Techniques*. For those of you who already have Books One and Two, we hope you will enjoy this book just as much and find it to be a good reference and resource from which to obtain ideas and inspiration.

Since Books One and Two were written, there have been many changes in styles of sugarcraft and, most importantly, the availability of equipment and products. These products have expanded our horizon to be able to produce all sorts of wonderful decorations. Many of these items have also been made to help the sugarcraft artist create cakes and decorations with more ease and less time.

I was very honoured to be asked to write this book and delighted when Margaret Ford agreed to co-author the book with me. Margaret and I, along with her husband David, have worked together a great deal, including many sugarcraft road shows and demonstrations; we have also produced a range of video tapes and the SugarFacts, which is a series of files on different elements of sugarcraft, along with some video-assisted material.

Margaret and I have very similar ideas about what we like to create in sugarcraft. Between us, we have also developed some teaching techniques and materials that we both use in our everyday teaching, including the size guide. This method has been adopted by thousands of sugarcraft artists around the world as a way of being able to measure a piece of paste to achieve perfect and consistent sizes for modelling rose cones, flower buds and many other items.

In planning this book, we wanted to open up its scope by including guest authors. We felt this would add to the appeal of the book and the styles of each of our work. The logistics of scheduling photography and writing a book on three continents had challenging moments, and we hope you will be pleased with the result. We feel this is a very balanced book with something for everyone, and hope you will enjoy creating many of the cakes and items included.

Margaret Ford   Nicholas Lodge

Margaret Ford Margaret first discovered her interest in cake decorating at catering college in Aberdeen and subsequently expanded her skills alongside a master baker. She began to design original and innovative equipment and, about 10 years ago, with her husband David, created the CelCakes (C) specialist range of products – the yellow CelPad, for example, has become an essential in a cake decorator's workbox. Margaret has travelled extensively in the UK and overseas demonstrating her skills. She regularly visits the USA and Holland, but has also taught in South Africa, Australia, New Zealand, Japan, Hong Kong and Argentina.

Nicholas Lodge Since writing Books 1 and 2, Nicholas has continued travelling around the world teaching and demonstrating sugarcraft. In 1991, he moved to live in Atlanta, Georgia, USA, where he set up the International Sugar Art Collection (ISAC). Along with his partner, Scott Ewing, he operates a school of confectionery and sugar arts, a retail cake decorating store, mail order and internet business.

In 1995, the International Sugar Art Gallery Japan was opened. This Tokyo based school and retail operation serve as the centre for Nicholas's Pacific Rim operations.

Nicholas is heavily involved in ICES (the International Cake Exploration Société) – an American based international convention that is held each year. In 2001, ICES inducted Nicholas into the Cake Decorating Hall of Fame. He is the youngest person that this honour has been bestowed upon.

June Twelves Starting as a teacher of international cookery, June soon developed a flair for cake decorating and sugarcraft and, combining a hobby of porcelain doll making with sugarcraft, June's love of modelling soon became apparent. She designed a range of moulds and modelling and texturing tools, and developed new innovative techniques designed to make modelling easy and enjoyable. Movement, detail and colour in the modelling soon led to numerous gold medals and requests for workshops and demonstrations involved travelling extensively in the UK, Ireland, the Channel Islands, Holland and the USA.

Marion Frost Marion Frost has worked in the bakery industry since leaving school. Gaining the City and Guilds Certificate and the 730 Teaching Certificate, she spent many years teaching sugarcraft in Liverpool. Marion opened a wedding cake studio and classroom, and has won many British Sugarcraft Guild Competitions at local and national level.

She is now a partner with husband Gerry in their cake decorating equipment business, Patchwork Cutters. She has written many books on the subject and has travelled to South Africa, America, Holland and Ireland, teaching and demonstrating her products.

Toshie Harashima Born in Tokyo, Japan, Toshie has been teaching sugarcraft for 15 years and has assisted in spreading sugarcraft throughout Japan. A manager and teacher at the Nicholas Lodge International Sugar Art Gallery in Tokyo, she demonstrates on NHK television programmes and at many exhibitions in Japan, England and South Africa. In the UK, she has been awarded many prizes including 'Best in Show' at the Sugarcraft & Cake Decoration Show 2000, silver award at Inspiration Creation 2001 of the British Sugarcraft Guild, and the Squires Kitchen Trophy. Toshie is a representative of Japan at ICES.

Earlene Moore Earlene has 40 years' experience as a cake decorator. She is a teacher, demonstrator, cake show judge and web page designer. An ICES charter member, past board member and past president (1987–88), Earlene now operates a small custom cake and specialty equipment business in Lubbock, Texas. She is an amateur photographer, taking pictures for her portfolio as well as her own web site.

Steven Stellingwerf Steven has been decorating cakes for over 30 years and teaching for over 20 years. He is an inductee of the Wilton President's Club and Wilton Hall of Fame. Steven has previously authored *The Gingerbread Book* and *Perfectly Simple Muffins*, and has been featured in a variety of books and magazines. Residing in Sioux Falls, South Dakota, he has travelled internationally and throughout the USA, teaching, judging and sharing the art of sugarcraft.

Moulds and cutters

Over the last few years the style of cake decorating has changed with the wider use of sugarpaste (rolled fondant). Those without a royal icing background, and the practice and development of piping techniques, are now able to create and produce effective traditional icing designs with the use of moulds and cutters. Because results can be achieved much more quickly, they allow more economical cake decorations for customers. Although the details may not be as finely finished, they are extremely effective and less time consuming.

Mould and cutter techniques

Although one disadvantage with moulding is that everyone could be producing the same decoration, moulds have been developed that allow the users to create smaller moulded elements and arrange and assemble them in individual ways. As a result, cake decorators achieve different effects from their various moulds, according to their own imagination and individual expression.

In this section, the techniques and variations in using the outline, lacework, lattice, snowflake and stamen moulds (C) are described. The stages of producing a really professional finish are carefully explained and, with a little imagination, can be extended to offer many more possibilities.

The method of making your own moulds is covered in detail, from how to make a single-sided mould and veiner to double-sided moulds, as well as the use of silicone moulds, using silicone plastique, and hard-resin moulds, showing their scope in sugarcraft. The cakes shown in this section each focus on a range of moulds or cutters. Marion Frost also demonstrates her innovative patchwork cutter technique.

1 The outline mould (C) is used with flower paste (gum paste). No cornflour (cornstarch) or vegetable fat is required. Press enough paste into the selected shape to adequately fill. Remove the excess with a fine palette knife, using a sawing action and working from the centre outwards. Take extra care to keep the blade flat to the mould surface, keeping pressure on the paste, to prevent it from slipping. Turn the mould around and repeat for the other side.

2 The mould can also be used with more than one colour of paste at any one time. For the rose, press pink flower paste into the petal part of the flower only and then trim excess away. Press green paste into the calyx area and then trim. Rub the surface well with a little vegetable fat on your finger and, using a large dressmaking pin, flick out the moulded piece.

3 For the lilac cake, keep the moulded pieces in a polythene bag so that they do not dry out. Smooth the surface of a freshly covered cake, then place the soft flowers and leaves in the desired pattern on top of the paste. Gradually press with a cake smoother until all the pieces are flush with the cake surface. The delicate bell motifs have been moulded in white, dried and brushed with powder colours, then attached to the cake.

4 Small individual cakes are very popular with less traditional brides. The outline shapes have all been worked in brown flower paste. To fill the outlines, colour sugarpaste (rolled fondant), soften it with water to a thick creamy consistency, and carefully fill individual sections from a piping bag without a tube (tip). Leave time for drying before adjacent areas are filled. A damp brush is useful for small detail. Alternatively, royal icing can be used for this technique.

5 Composite pictures can be made up by using several pieces from the mould. (Note: the rose outline was moulded in a slightly darker colour than the paste used to flood it in, whereas on the pansy, the purple colour was used to outline all the petals). When the flooded paste has dried, a second layer can be applied to give a more three-dimensional effect. Fine line work completes the design.

6 Trimming and removing items from the intricate snowflake mould (C) is similar to the outline mould. Extra care is needed where very fine multi-pointed shapes are removed. Several points or tips may need to be released with a pin before flicking the shape out of the mould. Pieces can be used flat, curved or cupped, and attached singly or in combinations to create a design.

7 Small individual pieces have been combined to create a doily effect. Mould the snowflake shapes in flower paste. Cut out a small square and larger circular ring in sugarpaste. The still-soft pieces can now be pressed between the sugarpaste outlines to create this design, which can be worked directly on to a cake or on to a parchment surface and left to dry. Brush the pieces lightly with a wet brush on the contact points of the pieces, if necessary.

8 Roll brown flower paste into a fine stalk and mould one each of the two sizes of snowflake in green. Cut and separate the individual spikes and use these to form the fronds of the spruce. Add tiny cones made by snipping a flower paste cone shape with scissors. For the Christmas tree, use halved snowflakes and pinch in the centre of each to progressively reduce their size.

9 Pieces from the lacework mould (C) can be used in the conventional way or combined to create various designs. In the third design panel, the lace edge is brushed with water. Attach while soft to a panel of sugarpaste, which has been embossed using a cuqui embosser M1 and dusted with powder colours.

10 If flowers are required without using any inedible materials, stamens can be moulded in flower paste. Trim away the excess paste, release several points and carefully remove from the mould with a pin. Centres can be placed on top of each other and cupped on sponge.

11 Lily stamens can be moulded in a similar way but need to be hung to dry before attaching to the flower. Remove these stamens from the mould, by pulling the joined end with thumb and forefinger. Dust with colour while still soft and then roll so that the pistil ends up in the centre with stamens around it. Drop the pistil through a supporting ring made from fine wire and leave to dry.

MAKING YOUR OWN MOULDS

1 To make silicone plastique moulds, mix equal parts of grey and blue compound in the desired amount by kneading well. Place on to a small plastic sheet and press the item to be moulded into it. Leave undisturbed for about 2 hours (depending on size), to cure. After curing, remove the original; the mould is now ready for use. Silicone plastique has a long shelf life but, once mixed, there is only a 10–15 minute working time, so only mix up what you can work with in that time.

2 Moulding jewellery, stones and decorative items is only one of the many uses of silicone plastique. Once mixed, roll out the silicone between plastic sheets, remove the top sheet of plastic and press the stone or decorative piece into the silicone. Leave for 2 hours. Remove and press flower paste into the mould. Remove and dry. To shine gemstones, use confectioner's glaze mixed with pearl or lustre dust. Paint the gold filigree design with gold powder and lemon extract.

3 For double-sided moulds, like the baby, press the silicone on to one side of the baby. Leave to cure for 2 hours, then brush dishwashing liquid around the edge of the cured piece. Mix up more silicone and press on to the other side to join the cured piece. Cure for 2 hours, then remove the two parts – the dishwashing liquid will stop the mould sticking together. Wash the mould before use, and dry. The other baby items shown can also be moulded.

4 For a single-sided petal or leaf veiner, roll out silicone between plastic. Remove the top sheet and press the leaf or petal into the silicone so that it sticks. Leave for 2 hours. For a double-sided veiner, initially make a single-sided veiner. Once cured, brush dishwashing liquid around the edge and press a fresh piece of silicone on top. Leave for 2 hours. Peel apart. Remove the leaf or petal, then wash the veiner before use.

5 There are many commercially available moulds that make very attractive decorations for a cake. Use flower paste or, on larger items like the squirrel shown, use a combination of flower paste and sugarpaste. For fine-detailed items like the forget-me-not ring, put the mould into the freezer for 15–20 minutes to firm the paste and then remove the item. This will stop any distortion. Once dry, the designs can be dusted or painted.

6 These hard-style decorative moulds were initially designed for use with polymer clays but work very well with edible mediums, such as sugarpaste, flower paste and marzipan. Here a winter village scene has been created using one of the house and church moulds from the extensive PM collection. Decorate the moulded houses using royal icing. Make small gingerbread men from cutters and use as accent decorations.

Springtime crocus cake

The fresh yellow colouring coupled with a crocus design on the sides gives this pretty cake a real springtime appearance. The intricate lacy lattice is made simply from a mould and trimmed to shape while soft.

COVERING THE CAKE

1 Brush the cake with apricot glaze, then cover with almond paste. When dry, brush the almond paste with clear alcohol and cover the cake and board with pale yellow sugarpaste (rolled fondant). Leave to dry.

2 With a pin, prick the top edge of the cake in the centre of each side and at each end.

LATTICE

3 Take a size 10 ball (see page 191) of white 50/50 sugarpaste/flower paste (gum paste) mix, then flatten and press into the lattice mould. There is no need to use cornflour (cornstarch) in the mould.

4 Using a fine palette knife, slice away the excess paste, working

Cake and Decoration

- 20cm (8in) oval cake
- apricot glaze
- 850g (1lb 14oz) almond paste
- clear alcohol (gin or vodka)
- 28cm (11in) oval cake board
- 1kg (2¼lb) pale yellow sugarpaste (rolled fondant)
- 200g (7oz) white flower paste (gum paste)
- 150g (5oz) white sugarpaste
- 3 crocus flowers, 2 buds and 5 leaves (see pages 136–137)
- lilac and green dusting powders
- small amount of softened green sugarpaste
- 1m (3ft), 15mm (½in) lilac ribbon

Special Equipment

- size guide (C)
- lattice mould (C)
- small fine palette knife
- 2 paper icing bags
- small crocus cutters (C)
- fine needle tool (C)
- small ball tool
- fine paintbrush
- no. 1 piping tube (tip)

■ While trimming the excess away, it is necessary to press firmly on to the surface of the paste.

■ By using a longer piece of paste and moving it along, it is possible to make a continuous strip of lattice.

Bend the part-dried lattice shape carefully before attaching the piece over the edge of the cake so that it fits close to the cake side.

For a neat finish, make sure that the edges of the lattice pieces are lined up to form a smooth curve all around the cake top. While soft, the lattice can be shaped very easily.

When cut down the middle, the lattice strip is attached partly to the cake base and partly to the board surface, so that both edges have a lacy effect.

towards you from the centre outwards, while holding the paste with fingers to prevent it from moving. Turn the mould around and remove the remaining excess paste in the same way. Smooth the trimmed surface with a finger before carefully peeling the lattice out. Trim away paste at the wide end. Lay the pieces over a paper piping bag to firm (but not dry). Four pieces are required.

LATTICE ASSEMBLY

5 Brush the narrow end and both sides of the lattice shape with water and attach one piece to each side and end of the cake. The top should be 1cm (1/2in) in from the cake edge.

6 Roll a size 11 ball of 50/50 paste to a length of 15cm (6in) and, working from one end, press it into the long narrow straight-sided design.

7 Trim away the excess paste, a small section at a time, while holding the paste firmly in the mould. Remember it is much easier to work towards you than away from you. Smooth the trimmed surface and then move on to another section.

8 Before trimming the final piece, carefully peel the lattice from the mould and place it back in again in a different position, so that the full length piece of paste can be moulded and trimmed, creating a piece that is longer than the mould itself. Four pieces are required.

9 Brush the back of each strip in turn with water and position it between the lattice pieces already on the cake. Trim the ends with a pair of scissors so that they fit neatly in place. Ensure that a smooth curve is formed on the cake top and sides.

10 Mould a strip long enough to go all the way around the base of the cake – about 64cm (24in). Using a palette knife or a pair of scissors, split the lattice strip lengthwise. Brush the underside of the wider piece with water and attach it to the board. Moisten the back of the narrower piece of lattice strip and attach it around the cake base. Join both at one end of the cake.

CROCUS

11 Roll out white flower paste and cut out petals (three per flower) with the small-sized crocus cutters. Vein the petals on one side only with the squared end of the needle tool, working from the centre outwards over the petal surface.

12 Place the petals on a soft foam surface and cup the reverse side of each petal with a small ball tool. Attach two petals together by overlapping them at the base and securing with edible glue. Place a third petal on top of these as shown. Trim neatly at the base.

13 When dry, dust with lilac dusting powder and add a touch of green at the base. Four pairs of these flower shapes are required.

FINISHING TOUCHES

14 Soften the pale yellow sugarpaste with water to piping consistency and place in a piping bag (no tube required). Attach the crocus design to the cake sides. Pipe lines above and below with softened green-coloured paste using a no. 1 piping tube (tip).

15 Pipe a green line around the board, just inside the edge, and also inside the top edge of the cake.

16 To complete the cake, arrange and attach crocus buds, flowers and leaves to the cake surface with softened sugarpaste. Add a paste bow to complete the cake (for instructions on making bows, see page 58). Attach lilac ribbon around the board edge.

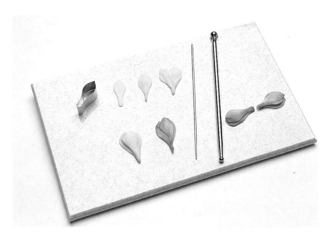

■ The smaller-sized crocus cutters are used to make a crocus design on the cake sides to complement the wired flowers on the top. Trim pieces at the base to ensure a neat fit.

■ Lines and spots piped in softened green-coloured paste on either side of the crocus flowers complete the side design. Use a damp paintbrush to neaten lines and spots.

USEFUL TIPS

• Dip a finger in vegetable fat to rub the trimmed paste surface.

• There is no need to start again if the lattice is incomplete. Just add a fresh piece of paste on top, rub well and trim.

• Long pieces can also be made by placing shorter pieces back in the mould, end to end, and adding extra paste over the join. Rub well to integrate the icing and trim to give an invisible join.

■ A matching fine green line is piped just inside the board edge and the lattice trim before attaching the wired crocuses on the top. The cake is finished with a paste ribbon.

Hexagonal wedding cake

This elegant wedding cake, though covered in sugarpaste, has the appearance of a royal iced cake with runout collar pieces, and is formal in design. The Celtic pattern and moulded borders could be substituted with other designs.

COVERING THE CAKES AND BOARDS

1 Brush the cakes with apricot glaze, then cover with almond paste. When dry, brush the almond paste with clear alcohol. It is important that the top edges are well defined when the cake is covered with sugarpaste (rolled fondant). To ensure this, firstly cover the top of the cakes, trim neatly and allow to dry. Cover the sides and trim to give a neat join on the top edge.

2 To match the colour of flower paste (gum paste) to the cake covering, mix white dusting powder with a small amount of vegetable fat to break down the granules and then work into the flower paste.

Cake and Decoration

- 28cm (11in) and 18cm (7in) hexagonal cakes
- apricot glaze
- 2.25kg (4lb 8oz) almond paste
- clear alcohol (gin or vodka)
- 2.5kg (5lb 8oz) white sugarpaste (rolled fondant)
- 250g ($8^3/4$oz) 50/50 sugarpaste/flower paste (gum paste) mix
- white dusting powder
- 38cm (15in), 33cm (13in) and 23cm (9in) hexagonal cake boards
- 3.3m (11ft), 14mm ($^1/2$in) wide soft white ribbon
- softened sugarpaste

Special Equipment

- rounded border mould F-56 (RVO)
- dressmaking pin
- piping bag
- no. 1.5 piping tube (tip) (PME)
- Celtic mould S F-51 (RVO)
- Celtic mould L F-52 (RVO)
- 10cm (4in) polystyrene dummy, 6cm ($2^1/2$in) deep
- 10cm (4in) circle of parchment paper
- 2 x 5cm (2in), 4 x 2.5cm (1in) styrofoam balls
- small Amaco daisy mould (C, ISAC)

Press the trimmed paste well into the mould so that the tiny flower pattern becomes embossed on to the paste surface. Check the cut edge for neatness.

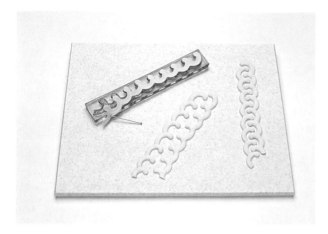

After each of the shapes has been moulded, it is necessary to allow them to partly dry interlinked so that they will fit together when placed on the cake.

When placing the outer trim on to the cake edge, it may be necessary to use soft sponge as a support until the icing dries completely. The sponge can then be removed.

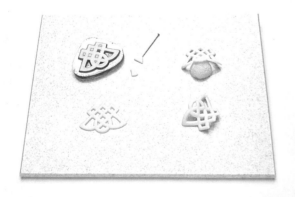

Small cutout pieces of paste can be removed easily with a dressmaking pin. Do not allow the pieces to dry out completely before attaching them to the cake.

3 Cover all the cake boards with sugarpaste and leave to dry. Place the cakes on the boards using two boards for the large cake. Attach the white ribbon around all three cake boards.

BORDER MOULDS

4 Dust both parts of the rounded border moulds with cornflour (cornstarch). Roll out 50/50 flower paste/sugarpaste, not too thinly, and lay this on top of one of the moulds. Press firmly into the design with fingers or a piece of soft sponge.

5 Roll over the surface with a small rolling pin to cut out the design. Rub the cutting edge with fingers to ensure a clean cut. Remove the paste carefully, trying not to stretch it. Mould the matching piece in the same way, then straighten both pieces and place together to partly dry on a flat surface.

6 Pipe softened sugarpaste on to the back of one piece using the no. 1.5 piping tube (tip) then place it on the board surface close to the edge of the cake. Continue working around the cake sides, trimming the ends to fit together. Attach the matching pieces, trimming in the same way. Joins can be neatened with softened sugarpaste piped into the small gaps.

7 When attaching the pieces to the cake top, support them, if necessary, with pieces of soft foam, which can be removed when dry.

CELTIC MOULDS

8 Dust the small Celtic mould with cornflour and place the paste over the top. Roll over the surface and remove the excess paste. Support the pieces in a curved shape over halved styrofoam balls (or other suitable shape).

9 Cover the sides of the cake dummy with a strip of sugarpaste and, when dry, place it on top of the circle of parchment in the centre of the larger cake.

10 Attach one partly dried shape to the centre of each cake side and around the cake separator with softened sugarpaste.

CAKE-TOP ORNAMENT

11 For the cake-top ornament, mould paste in the large Celtic shape and remove the excess as for the small one. Place the shape evenly over a large styrofoam ball until dry, then remove carefully. Three 'half-ball' pieces are required.

DAISIES

12 Dust the small daisy mould lightly with cornflour and place a small piece of paste into the shape. Do not overfill, bringing the excess paste to the centre back of the flower, leaving the petal tips neatly filled. Ease the paste out of the mould by gripping the mound of paste, which can then be trimmed away to leave a flat back. Eight daisies are required.

FINISHING TOUCHES

13 Match the two halves to create a ball shape, pipe a small amount of softened sugarpaste at the points where they meet and attach still-soft daisy shapes over the joins.

14 When dry, place the completed ball on to the remaining half-ball shape, securing with a small disc of soft 50/50 sugarpaste and flower paste, and piped sugarpaste.

15 Secure the top decoration to the centre of the small cake, adding extra daisies at the base.

USEFUL TIPS

• Trim any rough edges on moulded pieces with a craft knife.

• A fresh piece of 50/50 paste can be used to lift paste out of the moulds instead of a pin. Simply touch the surface of moulded paste with the fresh piece, press gently and lift away again. The shape should lift out of the mould easily.

To check for spacing, place the shapes all the way around the polystyrene separator before attaching. The same shaped pieces are attached to each cake side.

The Celtic design of this mould lends itself beautifully to creating the ball-shaped cake top ornament. Handle the pieces carefully when dry to avoid breakages.

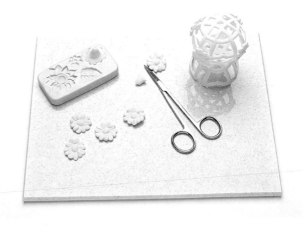

When the moulded daisies are attached to the ball shape, ensure that the halves are well secured together. The soft daisies can be curved to provide a larger area of contact.

Fantasy under the water

This delightful fantasy-style cake was inspired by the tales of Poseidon's lost city, Atlantis, and Neptune. On a project like this, your imagination can take over and this cake could be used for many different celebrations.

COVERING THE BOARD AND CAKE

1 To cover the board, roll out pale teal sugarpaste (rolled fondant.) Moisten the cake board using a little edible glue or piping gel. Cover the board, trim off excess paste and dry for several hours.

2 Cover the large cake first in dark cream paste and place on to the prepared board. Brush a mixture of cream food colouring and clear alcohol over the cake surface. Add a little dark brown to the cream colour and brush over the cake to highlight. Sponge the board using a natural sea sponge with a mixture of teal green and royal blue mixed with clear alcohol.

Brush a colour wash over the cake using a pastry brush and a mixture of cream food colouring and clear alcohol (gin or vodka).

Cake and Decoration

- 57cm (22in) wooden or cake board
- 750g (1lb 10oz) pale teal sugarpaste (rolled fondant)
- 40 x 10cm (16 x 4in), 15 x 8cm (6 x 3in), 13 x 10cm (5 x 4in), 10 x 15cm (4 x 6in) cakes
- 2.75kg (6lb) dark cream sugarpaste
- cream, dark brown, teal green, royal blue, moss green and orange food colourings
- clear alcohol (gin or vodka)
- 40cm (16in), 15cm (6in), 13cm (5in) and 10cm (4in) thin boards
- 1kg (2^1/4lb) white sugarpaste
- flower paste (gum paste)
- super pearl dusting powder
- orchid pink, cantaloupe, super green, teal and antique silk lustre dusts
- 2m (6^1/2ft), 1cm (^{1}/2in) wide peach ribbon

Special Equipment

- natural sea sponge
- 6mm, 8mm and 13mm bead maker (CK)
- no. 55 piping tube (tip) (AT)
- 20cm (8in) styrofoam cone and 8cm (3in) balls
- flower former
- dot-textured roller (RVO)
- fine tweezers
- silicone shell moulds (SB)
- silicone plastique (ISAC)

Add a little brown to the cream mixture and brush to give highlights. For the cake board, sponge a mixture of teal green and royal blue mixed with clear alcohol (gin or vodka) on to the board.

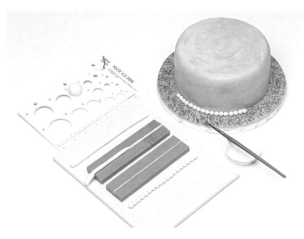

The edible pearls are made using a bead-maker mould. These go around all of the cakes and once attached are painted using super pearl dust mixed with clear alcohol to give an iridescent look.

The seaweed is piped using moss green royal icing and a no. 55 ribbon piping tube (tip). The seaweed is piped in a random pattern up the sides of all of the cakes.

3 Place the 10cm (4in) cake on to the 10cm (4in) thin board. To cover, roll out a strip of sugarpaste to wrap around the cake like a bandage, trimming the back to give a neat seam. Roll out more paste, cut out a 10cm (4in) disk and place this on top of the cake to seal it. Position this cake on the larger cake using some softened sugarpaste, positioning the seam at the back of the cake.

PEARLS

4 Taking equal amounts of white sugarpaste and flower paste (gum paste), make pearls by rolling a sausage of paste the length of the 13mm (1/2in) bead mould. Dust using cornflour (cornstarch), open up the mould and place the paste into the centre. Press the mould edges back together and trim off excess paste using a mini palette knife. Carefully remove the pearls from the mould. Brush a little edible glue around the base of the large and small cake and attach pearls around, joining them in sections as needed.

5 Cover the other two cakes and place on thin boards. Position as shown and attach pearls around the base of these cakes. (The pearls around all of the cakes are 13mm (1/2in) in size.) Mix some super pearl dusting powder with clear alcohol and paint over the pearls to give an iridescent look.

SEAWEED AND SHELLS

6 Pipe seaweed using moss green royal icing and a no. 55 ribbon tube (tip). Pipe in a random design and pattern on each cake.

7 For the large pointed shell, cover a 20cm (8in) styrofoam cone, or sculpted cake, with sugarpaste. Roll sausages of sugarpaste and press a flower former on top to mould into shape. Place the cone on a small cardboard, brush with edible glue and attach the moulded pieces around the cone, working in a spiral shape from bottom to top. Mark lines using a knife tool. Dry a little then, using orchid pink lustre dust and clear alcohol, paint this all over the shell. Mix cantaloupe lustre dust and alcohol, then paint in blocks over the shell. Dry a little, then attach 8mm (1/3in) pearls around the shell. Paint with super pearl mixed with alcohol.

8 The sea urchin can be made from a 8cm (3in) styrofoam ball, with each end cut off, or a muffin or cupcake. Cover with sugarpaste to give the basic shape, then roll out some pale moss green sugarpaste, roll over using the dot-textured roller. Brush edible glue over the urchin and carefully cover over the shape, trying not to lose the detail from the roller. Trim off excess paste, hollow the centre using a medium pin and pinch ridges using fine tweezers. Dry a little, then paint all over using super green lustre dust mixed with alcohol. Let dry a little more, then dust teal lustre dust to give blue highlights. Place on to a thin board, stick on to the cake and place 6mm (1/4in) pearls around the base. Paint the pearls as before.

9 The nautilus shell is made using the same centre as the sea urchin but it is used on its side. Roll out sugarpaste in a shape like a Concorde and brush edible glue over the centre. Roll up from the point to create a spiral shape as shown. Trim off excess paste and, using a knife tool, make markings on the shell. Dry a little and brush all over using antique silk lustre dust mixed with clear alcohol. Dry a little, then paint lines on to the shell using a mixture of cream, dark brown and orange. Dry and position on the cake.

FINISHING TOUCHES

10 Make various shells, sea creatures and fish using commercially available moulds or those made from silicone plastique (see page 14). Make smaller items from flower paste and larger items from a mixture of equal quantities of sugarpaste and flower paste. (It is a good idea to have real shells or photographs to copy colour and form.) Paint them in colours of your choice. Once dry, attach these items in position on the cake. Attach the peach-coloured ribbon around the cake-board edge.

Cover a styrofoam cone or sculpted cake with sugarpaste (rolled fondant), then spiral and attach rolled strips around, marking with a knife tool to give a natural look to the shell.

Cover the sea urchin using a dot-textured roller pattern, pinched using tweezers. Roll a Concorde shape of sugarpaste around the nautilus shell. Once dry, these are both painted using lustre dusts.

An assortment of commercially available moulds, and some made from silicone plastique, are used for the shells, sea creatures and fish. These are painted using various colours of lustre dust.

Shades of peach

This pretty cake is decorated in shades of one colour to give a very soft appearance. Adorned with lace and a butterfly settled on a chrysanthemum, this peach single-tier cake has a very feminine look.

Cake and Decoration

- 20cm (8in) round cake, about 8cm (3in) deep
- apricot glaze
- 750g (1lb 10oz) almond paste
- clear alcohol (gin or vodka)
- 27.5cm (11in) round cake board
- 750g (1lb 10oz) peach sugarpaste (rolled fondant)
- peach paste food colouring
- 100g (3¹/₂oz) flower paste (gum paste)
- small amount of royal icing
- peach dusting powder

Special Equipment

- lace mould (CK 1601)
- fine palette knife
- cake smoother
- strip of paper, 70 x 8cm (28 x 3in)
- nos. 1, 1.5 and 4 piping tubes (tips) (PME)
- several large dressmaking pins
- chrysanthemum petal cutters (C)
- fine needle tool
- shallow cup-shaped formers (medium and large) (C)
- size guide
- butterfly lace mould (CK 1489)
- 2 fine white stamens

LACE PIECES

1 Prepare and dry lace pieces before covering the cake if you wish to inlay the pieces. Alternatively, cover the cake and allow the surface to firm before attaching the lace pieces on top.

2 Dust the lace mould top and bottom with cornflour (cornstarch). Roll out a small piece of flower paste (gum paste) very thinly and place into the left-hand side of the mould. Cover with the top part of the mould and press firmly all over, especially around the edges. Tear away any excess paste while holding down the mould top firmly.

3 Remove the top piece, neaten the edge by pressing any excess back into the mould then, while holding carefully, remove the paste from the background areas with a small palette knife. These are the flat areas which are uppermost when the paste is still in the mould. Turn the mould over on the work surface and bend back slightly to release the paste. Thirteen well-dried pieces are required to go around the

■ It is important to use very thinly rolled paste so that the excess tears away easily and the design remains delicate.

■ Use a fine palette knife, not a sharp craft knife, so that the silicone mould is not damaged.

■ The lace pieces can be inlaid into the soft cake covering or simply attached to the dry sugarpaste surface, whichever method is preferred. Position the pieces in a circle.

■ Attach two spacers, in the same positions, to the back of each lace piece so that they will not be noticeable from the front when attached to the side of the cake.

■ Insert the supporting pins at a slightly upward angle to the cake side to prevent the lace sliding down before the securing icing has set. On removing the pins, no holes should be visible.

cake, and four extra pieces are needed for the inlay. Carefully trim these shapes while soft. Neaten the edges and leave to dry.

DECORATING THE CAKE

4 Cover the cake board with peach sugarpaste (rolled fondant). Brush the cake with apricot glaze and cover with almond paste. When dry, brush with clear alcohol, then cover with peach sugarpaste. Position the dried trimmed lace pieces in an evenly spaced circular pattern around the top. Use a cake smoother to gently press them into the soft covering until they are inlaid into the surface. Make sure that the cake top is smooth before leaving to dry.

5 Measure the circumference and height of the cake and prepare a paper collar to fit around the cake. Divide the length into 13 sections – about 7cm ($2^3/4$in). Draw a line along the length of the paper 3cm ($1^1/4$in) down from the top. Secure the paper collar around the cake and use a pin to mark the cake side where vertical and horizontal lines meet. Remove the paper.

6 Roll out a piece of flower paste to about 2mm ($1/12$in) in thickness and, using a no. 4 piping tube (tip), cut out small spacers. Remove each one individually from the tube by pushing with a pin. Two spacers are required for each lace piece (26 in total). Pipe two small spots of royal icing on to the back of the lace piece and, using a pin, lift each soft spacer and place on the royal icing. Leave to dry.

7 Insert a pin into each mark on the cake side. Pipe a small amount of royal icing onto the end of both spacers on the back of each lace piece. Using a pin to support them, attach the lace pieces to the side of the cake and leave to dry before removing the pins.

8 Pipe a snail's trail around the cake base using a no. 1.5 tube and matching royal icing.

FLOWER

9 Using flower paste the same colour as the lace pieces, roll out and cut out the petals for the chrysanthemum flower using the cutters. You will need 20 of the largest size, seven of the second size and eight of the smallest size. Place the cutter partly on some of the smallest ones and cut again to make smaller petals. Vein and stretch all the petals by rolling from side to side with the squared end of the fine needle tool. Curve the petals gently and place to dry in the medium flower former.

10 When dry, place parchment paper in the base of a large shallow former, pipe royal icing in the centre and attach the petals in rows, working towards the centre.

11 Before adding the smallest petals, take a size 6 ball of peach sugarpaste, flatten on the base and texture the top using the no. 1 piping tube. Place this piece in the centre of the flower and insert the small petals around the soft centre. Leave in the former to dry.

BUTTERFLY

12 Prepare and mould the wings as for the lace pieces and lay flat until quite dry. For the body, roll a size 4 ball of flower paste to a carrot shape about 2cm (³/4in) long. Use a pin to indent around the wide end to form the head and body. Mark across the body several times with a craft knife. Insert two stamens, dipped in gum glue, to 1.5cm (⁵/8in) in length to represent the feelers.

13 Cut a 1cm (¹/2in) square of flower paste and attach the body to it. Leave to dry. Attach the wings to this with royal icing and support with foam pieces.

14 Dust the flower and butterfly with peach before attaching them to the centre of the cake.

USEFUL TIPS

• Look carefully at the moulded pieces before use to determine which are the background areas.

• When using piping tubes as mini cutters, brush the tube with white vegetable fat (shortening) so that it is easier to remove the paste cutouts.

Pipe a snail's trail in matching coloured royal icing around the cake using a no. 1.5 piping tube. If you have a turntable it can be used for this stage.

After cutting out petals, assemble the flower, using royal icing, in shallow formers and leave supported until completely dry. Remove the parchment from the flower before placing on the cake.

Moulded wings can be made lacy by using a piping tube to cut out small additional holes. Dust the butterfly with peach dusting powder before placing on the cake.

GUEST AUTHOR

MARION FROST

Cutter Techniques

Using cutters for quick and easy cake designs
enables the cake decorator to produce a professional
finish, time after time. By using a different cutter,
the same technique can be used for different
occasions – for example, instead of a rose on
the overpiped outlines opposite, use a vintage car
cutter for a man's cake.

Overpiping: This technique, which also includes simple painting, can be used on a plaque as shown here, or applied directly on to a sugarpaste (rolled fondant) cake.

To make an oval plaque, knead together 115g (4oz) sugarpaste and 115g (4oz) Mexican paste (see page 186). Roll out and cover a 20 x 15cm (8 x 6in) oval cake board. Smooth evenly and trim the edges.

Grease a tea rose embosser with white vegetable fat (shortening), position on to the plaque and press firmly. Reposition the embosser and press firmly again. Remove the embosser and leave the plaque to dry thoroughly for about 24 hours.

Mix Christmas red dusting powder and a little clear alcohol, then paint the rose and bud using a no. 3 paintbrush. Mix holly/ivy green dusting powder and clear alcohol, then paint the leaves and stems.

Using a no. 2 piping tube (tip) and 50g (2oz) royal icing, pipe an even line into the embossed outlines. Leave the plaque to dry completely before adding the gold colour.

Mix brilliant gold dusting powder and alcohol, then paint the piped outline.

First paint the embossed flowers and then the leaves using a mixture of dusting powder and clear alcohol mixed in a small dish or paint palette.

Overpipe the embossed outline of the flowers and leaves using royal icing. Use a damp brush to tap down any high take-off points.

Using a no. 3 paintbrush, paint the dried overpiping with a mixture of gold dusting powder and clear alcohol. Care should be taken to cover all the piped outline.

Remove the completed plaque from the board and transfer to a cake, securing with a little royal icing. Overpiping also looks effective painted silver for anniversary cakes.

Cutter flowers: This section shows how to use individual flowers and leaves from a cutter to form your own arrangement.

Make a plaque as on page 33. For the flowers, using dusting powder or paste colours, colour small pieces of Mexican paste fern green, marigold orange, soft green and daffodil yellow. Roll out the fern green paste. Press the holly on the winter garland cutter on to the paste and press firmly. Remove the cutter, re-grease and reposition on to the paste and make 20 pieces of holly. Repeat using orange paste for 3 Chinese lanterns and white paste for Christmas roses.

Use soft green for 5 ivy leaves and yellow for 10 winter jasmine flowers and buds. To soften the edges of the winter roses and ivy leaves, place on a sponge pad and press a celstick along the edge of each flower and leaf. Dust darker shades on to the flowers. Brush a little ruby on the Christmas roses edges before overdusting with white satin.

Using green and ruby dusting powders and alcohol, paint green and ruby stems, and green leaf sprays on to the plaque. Use sugarpaste mixed with water to attach the flowers and leaves. Roll balls of red sugarpaste for holly berries. Attach and paint a dot of bulrush colour on to each berry.

On a greased non-stick board, cut flowers and leaves from coloured Mexican paste, using the cutter greased with white vegetable fat. Remove excess paste. Dry on a sponge pad.

Flowers and leaves must be dry before painting or dusting. Dust darker shades on to the dry flowers and leaves. Mix fern green dusting powder and alcohol and paint the ivy.

Cut out extra stems freehand from green Mexican paste. Attach and stick with a moist no. 2 brush. Arrange the dried flowers once the stems and fine leaves have been painted on.

Cover a 25 x 20cm (10 x 8in) cake with 900g (2lb) green sugarpaste. Stipple using a damp sponge and soft green powder. Secure the plaque to the cake with a piped border.

Figures: There are a huge variety of cutters for figures, providing all kinds of cakes for everyone.

Colour small pieces of Mexican paste bulrush, grey using blackberry, daffodil and fern green using dusting powders. Roll out brown Mexican paste. Cut out the hedgehog using the cutter. Repeat using grey paste for the mouse cutter, fern green and white for the cauliflower cutter, etc. from the vegetable cutter set.

First paint the vegetables, then continue with the figures. Mix bulrush powder and alcohol and paint the hedgehog spines. Paint orange shoes and a pastel pink nose. Cut out and place pea pods on to the hand area. Cut out an extra arm and stick to the hedgehog with water. Dust darker grey powder around the mice from the outside edge inwards using a no. 6 brush. Dry dust pastel pink cheeks and fingertips. Paint pink ears. Cut out an extra arm or hands to hold the vegetables.

Cover a 15 x 20cm (6 x 8in) plaque with white sugarpaste (rolled fondant). Dust the top half peach and the lower half green. Attach a sausage of white sugarpaste across the centre and moisten.

For the tablecloth, cut out white sugarpaste strips 5cm (2in) deep, then gather and attach on to the sausage of sugarpaste. Attach vegetables.

On a greased non-stick board, roll out Mexican paste and cut out figures and vegetables in appropriate colours using cutters greased with white vegetable fat. Dry on a sponge pad.

Leave all pieces to dry before painting. With a no. 3 paintbrush, paint detail on to the vegetables and figures using dusting powders and alcohol mixed in a paint palette.

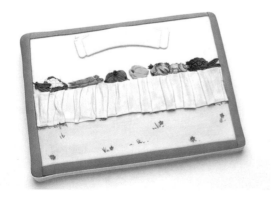

Using sugarpaste softened with water to form a stiff glue, stick the tablecloth and vegetables to the plaque. Cut out the banner using the cutter and attach to the plaque.

Cut out small flowers taken from the mini flowers squares set and position. Add the mice and hedgehog figures to complete the plaque. Add an inscription to the banner.

Side designs: These are important to cake design. *Gardening* – Cut out a strip of paper 8cm (3in) deep to fit around the cake. Fold into 6 equal sections. Fold into 8 sections for a square cake. Draw a curved line on the paper between the top two corners. Cut along the line making a scalloped edge. Secure this template around the cake with tape. Use a cocktail stick (toothpick) to mark the curved edge. Remove the template.

Colour small pieces of Mexican paste using marigold, daffodil, leaf green and bulrush dusting powders. Roll out green paste and cut out 6–8 boots from the fisherman cutter. Cut out vegetables in appropriate colours. Paint the vegetables. Dust lime green at the base of the celery. Dry dust dark green around the boots. Attach the pieces to the marked guidelines.

DIY – Cover a round or square cake with baby blue sugarpaste. Emboss the cake sides with the square grid from the squares set. Knead 115g (4oz) Mexican paste and 115g (4oz) sugarpaste to make stencil paste. Colour half with hyacinth blue.

Grease the selected cutter and cut out dark blue squares. Moisten the squares on the cake sides with water and attach.

Attach the pre-cut and coloured DIY tools.

On a lightly greased non-stick board, cut out the vegetables from the vegetable cutter set and boots only from the fisherman cutter. Place on a sponge pad to dry.

Transfer the dry pieces to a firm board, then paint and dust the boots, vegetables and tools in appropriate colours and shades, using a no. 3 paintbrush.

On a greased non-stick board, roll out white and blue stencil paste for side squares using the squares set and white Mexican paste for DIY tools. Trim the hammer to fit the square.

Attach the pieces on to the cake side using sugarpaste softened with water, repeating the pattern. These side decorations can be adjusted to suit any shape of cake.

Painted cross stitch effects: By following cross stitch patterns, the theme for this technique can be altered. This finished plaque could become the front cover of a pastillage book or card.

Roll out 115g (4oz) white Mexican paste. Firmly press the embroidery grid embosser on to the paste. Remove and trim the edge. Leave to dry.

Mix chiffon pink dusting powder and alcohol to form a painting solution. Divide into three equal amounts. Add sufficient white satin powder to lighten two, producing three shades of pink.

Count the squares to centralise your chosen embroidery pattern. Begin with the top squares and, following the pattern down, paint a small dot of colour on to the centre of each square. Change shades and colours as the pattern indicates.

Roll out 115g (4oz) white Mexican paste. Well grease the lace cutter from the squares set and press firmly on to the paste. Remove the cutter. Use a cocktail stick (toothpick) to pick out small centre pieces. Repeat the cutting out process and place the second piece of lace against the first making a centre seam. Using a 1cm ($^1/_2$in) serrated straight crimper, crimp along the centre seam on the lace. Attach the lace and dust.

Press the lightly greased embroidery grid embosser on to white Mexican paste and trim around the outside edge leaving a narrow border.

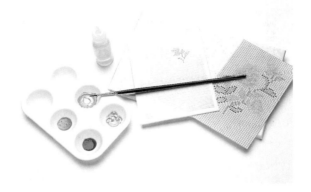

Following your chosen pattern, paint tiny dots of colour on to the grid using a mix of clear alcohol and dusting powder and a no. 000 paintbrush.

On a lightly greased non-stick board, cut lace pieces from Mexican paste, removing surplus paste. Attach two rows back to back. Crimp along the centre seam.

Moisten the narrow border on the embroidery grid with water and carefully attach the lace. Brush with white satin dusting powder.

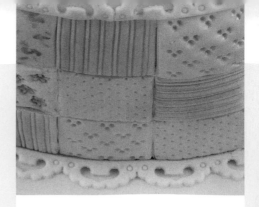

Patchwork cake

Although this pretty cake is suitable for all ages, it is ideal for first birthdays, especially if the mouse is holding a present. It is also the perfect celebration cake for a patchwork or needlework enthusiast.

_____

PATCHWORK DECORATION

1 Brush the cake with apricot glaze and cover with the almond paste. Brush the almond paste with clear alcohol, then cover the cake with the pink sugarpaste (rolled fondant).

2 Emboss the squares grid from the squares set on to the cake sides. The final row of squares may be made larger or smaller as necessary. Leave to dry.

3 Cover the cake board with a strip of sugarpaste and smooth over the join.

Cake and Decoration

- 20cm (8in) round cake
- apricot glaze
- 900g (2lb) almond paste
- clear alcohol (gin or vodka)
- 900g (2lb) shell pink sugarpaste (rolled fondant)
- 28cm (11in) round cake board
- 225g (8oz) Mexican paste
- 50g (2oz) white sugarpaste
- chiffon pink, blackberry, white satin, myrtle, forget-me-not and daffodil dusting powders (SK)
- white vegetable fat (shortening)
- ribbon to trim cake board

Special Equipment

- squares set (PC)
- embroidery grid (PC)
- 9cm (3 1/2in) circle cutter
- mouse cutter (PC)
- paint palette
- no. 3 paintbrush
- no. 000 paintbrush

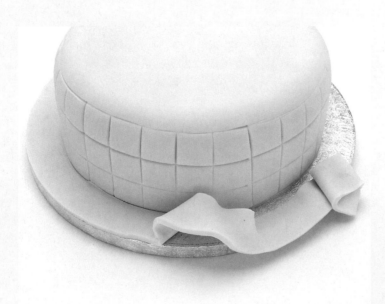

■ After embossing the cake sides with the square grid, cover the cake board with a strip of sugarpaste.

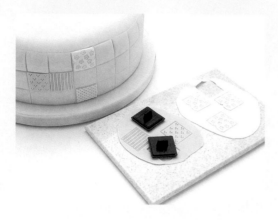

Cut out squares of pink and white stencil paste using the various designs available. Attach them on to the cake sides following the pre-embossed outline.

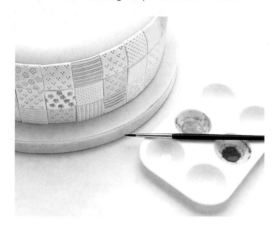

Paint in the patterns on the square designs using a paintbrush and pink dusting powder mixed with clear alcohol. Paint each flower completely.

Emboss the Mexican paste with the embroidery grid embosser. Cut out a 9cm (3¹/₂in) diameter circle and emboss with the mouse cutter.

4 Knead 115g (4oz) of pink sugarpaste and 115g (4oz) Mexican paste together to form a stencil paste. Colour half of this paste a slightly darker pink than the pink sugarpaste.

5 On a lightly greased non-stick board, roll out the pink stencil paste. Grease a single square-patterned cutter with white vegetable fat (shortening) and cut out squares.

6 Moisten an area on the cake with water and attach the cut-out square. Repeat using various patterns and shades of pink. Place striped squares both vertically and horizontally.

7 Make up white stencil paste with the 50g (2oz) white sugarpaste and 50g (2oz) Mexican paste. Cut out and attach white stencil paste squares approximately every fourth row. Trim the base squares slightly to fit the now shortened outline. Continue until all areas are complete.

8 Paint in flowers and stripes in shades of pink to highlight the different designs.

MOUSE PLAQUE

9 On a non-stick board, roll out white Mexican paste and emboss using the embroidery grid.

10 Cut out a 9cm (3¹/₂in) diameter circle and emboss the mouse cutter into the centre. Trim away excess paste and leave to dry.

11 Mix together blackberry and white satin dusting powders with clear alcohol. Paint all grey areas on the mouse, then paint a tail.

12 Mix the pink dusting powder with alcohol, then paint all pink areas. Add extra black to the grey colour and paint all shaded areas, adding more alcohol as necessary. Use black dusting powder and alcohol to paint the eyes and nose.

13 On a lightly greased non-stick board, roll out myrtle green Mexican paste, forget-me-not blue Mexican paste and chiffon pink Mexican paste. To make the bunch of flowers, cut a keyhole shape from the green paste,

cutting through the wide end to form flower stems.
Attach this to the mouse.

14 Using the flower square cutter, cut out pink and blue
flowers. Moisten the green base with water and attach the
flowers. Paint in tiny daffodil yellow centres.

FINISHING TOUCHES

15 Moisten the centre of the cake with water and place
the mouse plaque into position.

16 On a lightly greased non-stick board, thinly roll
out white Mexican paste. Liberally grease the lace cutter
from the squares set and press firmly on to the paste.
Remove and repeat. Lift out the small pieces with a
cocktail stick (toothpick). Remove excess paste.

17 Attach the lace strip around the moistened edge of
the plaque. Lift the lace at intervals with a paintbrush
handle to create an even flounce. Repeat, adding lace to
the top and bottom edges of the cake.

18 Attach ribbon around the cake-board edge, sticking
with a non-toxic glue stick.

■ Paint the mouse using appropriate dusting powder
colours mixed with clear alcohol. Leave to dry.
Highlights are lightly brushed on to the dried mouse.

■ Cut a keyhole shape from green Mexican paste.
Cut through the lower half to make stems. Use the
flower square to cut out flowers.

PROFESSIONAL TIPS

• Do not lift the Mexican paste from the board when rolling
out; this will ensure that the paste stays on the board and not
in the cutter when cutting out shapes.

• When cutting out small shapes, such as flowers, roll the Mexican
paste more thinly and use more grease on the cutter.

• Use hot soapy water and a soft brush to clean the cutters
after use.

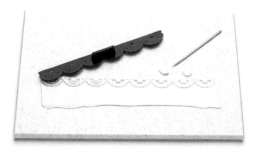

■ Cut out lace pieces using the lace cutter, remove the
small centre pieces. Attach the lace around the plaque
and the top and base of the cake.

Embossed wedding cake

This delightful cake carries a rose theme throughout, from the embossed cake design to the sugar flowers. The simple design is ideal for special anniversaries such as ruby and golden wedding celebrations.

EMBOSSING THE CAKES

1 Position each cake on to the centre of its board, placing the smallest cake on the smallest board, and so on. Brush the cakes with apricot glaze and cover with almond paste.

2 When dry, brush the almond paste with cooled boiled water or clear alcohol, then cover each cake and board with white sugarpaste (rolled fondant).

3 Smooth the sugarpaste and place the paper template on the top as shown. Secure with glass-headed pins. Using a cocktail stick (toothpick), scratch a line into the sugarpaste

Cake and Decoration

- 25cm (10in), 20cm (8in), and 15cm (6in) square cakes
- 30cm (12in), 25cm (10in) and 20cm (8in) square cake boards
- apricot glaze
- 2.75kg (6lb) almond paste
- clear alcohol (gin or vodka)
- 2.75kg (6lb) white sugarpaste (rolled fondant)
- white satin, dark green, burgundy, light green, lime green, yellow gold and brown dusting powders (SK)
- white vegetable fat (shortening)
- ribbon to trim cake boards
- 115g (4oz) green Mexican paste
- 175g (6oz) white Mexican paste
- spruce green food colour (SF)

Special Equipment

- 3 glass-headed pins
- cocktail stick (toothpick)
- wild rose cutter set (partly opened flower embosser) (PC)
- 1cm (1/2in) single-curved serrated crimper
- 2 x no. 3 paintbrushes
- 3 x no. 6 paintbrushes
- no. 000 paintbrush
- no. 2 piping tube (tip)

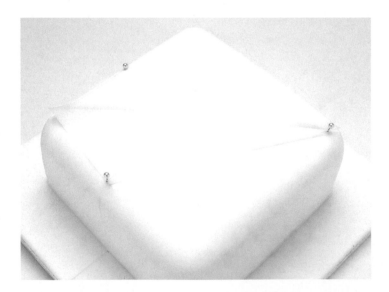

Pin a paper template on to the cake top. Following the template, scratch an outline using a cocktail stick. Continue down the sides and on to the board.

Emboss the pattern on the sugarpaste, keeping the design compact. Tip and press the embosser edge into small spaces, taking care not to overlap.

Using the single-curved serrated crimper, carefully crimp along the guide lines on the cake, pinching equally. Both rows of crimping face inwards.

Roll out green and white Mexican paste and cut out the required number of leaves, flowers and buds. Re-grease the cutter between each cut.

from the pointed end of the template to the pins. Continue down the cake sides and across the iced board. Remove the template and pins.

4 Use the partly opened flower embosser and begin at the narrowest end of the marked outline. Place the embosser on to the sugarpaste and press firmly. Remove the embosser, reposition as close to the first impression as possible and press firmly again. Continue until the whole area is embossed. Emboss any remaining small spaces with any part of the cutter that will fit the space. Avoid overlapping any embossed area.

5 Using the single-curved serrated crimper, crimp along the guide lines.

6 Brush over the embossed area with white satin dust, protecting the smooth areas with cling film (plastic wrap.) Leave to dry. Decorate all three cakes in the same way.

7 Use a glue stick to attach the ribbon around the cake boards.

FLOWERS AND LEAVES

8 On a lightly greased non-stick board, roll out the green Mexican paste.

9 Grease the leaf cutters from the wild rose cutter set, place on to the paste and press firmly. Reposition and repeat.

10 Place the leaves on to a sponge pad and soften around the edges using the rounded end of the celstick. Leave to dry.

11 Roll out the white Mexican paste and cut out the flowers and buds using the cutters. Soften the edges on the sponge pad using the celstick. Add extra foreground petals to the flower and bud, and attach while still soft. Leave to dry.

12 Dry-dust the leaves with dark green and burgundy dusting powders. Brush over with a little light green. Dry-dust a little burgundy around the outside edge of the petals, stroking the brush from the outside edge in towards the centre – this will give a softer appearance. Brush a little lime green into the flower centre and yellow gold into the centre of the lime green. Finish by mixing brown dusting powder and clear alcohol to paint tiny stamens following the embossed pattern.

FINISHING TOUCHES

13 Moisten and attach a cone of sugarpaste on to the corner of the cake, where the flowers will be positioned.

14 Soften a small piece of white sugarpaste by working and stretching with your fingers. Add water and mix thoroughly with a knife until the paste is soft and smooth and can easily be passed through a no. 2 piping tube (tip.) Pipe small bulbs of sugarpaste around the base of the cake, leaving the embossed areas plain.

15 Use the small palette knife to lift the flowers and leaves, then attach them on to the cone of icing. Secure with the remaining softened sugarpaste.

Soften the edges of the flower petals, including the extra petals, before attaching them on to the main flower. Dry flowers in a former for a cupped effect.

Dust the leaves, flowers and buds in appropriate colours. Using brown dusting powder mixed with alcohol, paint tiny stamens.

PROFESSIONAL TIPS

• Remove all loose dust colouring on flowers and leaves before arranging them on the cake.

• Always make spare leaves to fill in small gaps.

• Always use glass-headed pins as they are more easily found if misplaced.

Gently lifting with a small palette knife, arrange the roses and leaves on to the cone of icing in the corner of the cake. Attach with softened sugarpaste.

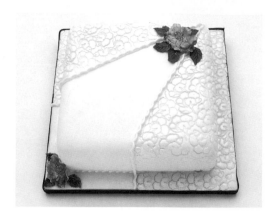

The flowers on the cake board can be replaced with decorative wedding rings to make a pretty single-tier wedding cake.

Use a darker shade of powder dusting colour on the embossed sections of the design to create an interesting colour contrast.

Arrange the flower spray across the embossed sections leaving sufficient space for names or celebrations to be written.

ALTERNATIVE EMBOSSING IDEAS

These attractive celebration cakes show a variety of designs using the same embossing techniques as used on the previous pages. By dividing the cakes into sections and choosing which ones to leave plain or emboss, interesting designs can be achieved. Repositioning the flowers or choosing another decoration, such as a bow, gives a completely different look.

Embossing different areas: Follow the instructions for the main wedding cake but emboss the outer sections instead, including the cake board. This will give a completely different look to the cake. Roll a thin length of sugarpaste (rolled fondant), attach to the guide lines and crimp with a 1cm (1/2in) single-curved serrated crimper. Use the roses from the main wedding cake, but use only two.

Choosing a different decoration: Divide the cake into four by marking guidelines across the sugarpaste. Emboss opposite sections and crimp the edges. Dust with chiffon pink dusting powder. Make a bow from embossed Mexican paste and gather the centres before drying the four pieces (see also page 53). Brush with pink dust and place the four dried pieces on to the cake. Attach a strip of embossed paste over the bow joins to form a centre ring. Roll a thin length of sugarpaste, attach around the base of the plain sections, and crimp.

Embossing opposite corners: Divide the cake into four, then emboss opposite sections and crimp the edges as before. Dust the embossed sections with white satin dusting powder. A wired spray of leaves and flowers can be used as a centre decoration as an alternative to the bow. Ideal for a double celebration, such as a birthday and anniversary, or for two people sharing, for example, twins' birthday or a christening.

This simple cake is ideal for a ruby wedding anniversary. Use different colours for a golden anniversary, engagement, wedding or Valentine's Day celebration. The same instructions apply for any shaped cake.

Brush a 20cm (8in) heart-shaped cake with apricot glaze. Cover with 900g (2lb) almond paste. Leave to dry. Cover a 25cm (10in) heart cake board and the sides of the cake with 450g (1lb) ruby sugarpaste (rolled fondant).

Moisten the top of the cake with clear alcohol and cover with 450g (1lb) white sugarpaste. Allow the white sugarpaste to overlap the ruby sugarpaste. Trim away excess white paste approximately half-way down the sides of the cake.

Emboss the white section of the cake with a wild rose cutter.

Using a lace cutter from the square set, cut out and attach lace pieces along the join where the white and ruby pastes meet.

Cover the ruby-coloured section with cling film (plastic wrap) and brush the white section liberally with white satin dusting powder. Remove the cling film.

Position sugar or silk roses and leaves on the cake board and cake top. Attach ribbon to the cake board using a non-toxic glue stick.

Carefully cover the cake board and sides of the heart-shaped, almond paste-covered cake with ruby sugarpaste. Soften the cut edge around the cake sides.

Cover the top of the cake with white sugarpaste, overlapping at the sides. Cut away excess white paste half-way down the cake, leaving a neat finish.

Dust the embossed cake with white satin dusting powder, then add flowers to the cake top and board. A small gift tag can be added with an inscription.

PROFESSIONAL TIPS

• Do not roll out dark sugarpaste (rolled fondant) on icing sugar as this will dull and cloud the finish. Roll out on a greased surface.

• Dried out or skinned sugarpaste can be softened by placing the unwrapped sugarpaste in an airtight box with a whole lemon. Test the icing every 2 hours.

Fabric effects

Interior designs, and the texture of the fabrics used in their making, act as a real inspiration for cake designers. Folds and gathers found in curtain drapes and other soft furnishings lend themselves well to being reproduced in sugar, often creating a soft romantic finish popular with brides. Different bows, tassels and other accents, together with the variety of equipment available for transferring textures on to the surface of sugarpaste (rolled fondant), create a wide range of possibilities for any cake decorator who is well prepared to respond to the changes in fashion.

Fabric effect techniques

The following section shows many ideas where the texture and finish of fabric has inspired a variety of techniques suitable for transference into cake design. It is important that the effect achieved has the soft appearance of gathered and folded fabric.

Combinations of several different finishes can be used, for example, on the gift packages cake, creating a pretty finish for a fairly simple design. There is frequent reference to the use of a pasta machine, which is a very useful piece of equipment when creating fabric effects. The use of a pasta machine ensures uniform thickness when making the long thin strips of paste required for drapes, bows and ribbons. Various types of pasta machines are available – from a basic hand-cranked model to machines with electric motors and models that fit as an attachment on to heavy duty mixers. When trying to mimic the appearance of fabric in sugarpaste, one of the most important factors is the thickness of the paste. The secret is to use thinly rolled out paste to achieve neat gathers and drapes without any trace of stiffness.

1 There are many different rolling pins or rollers available to create fabric textures on sugarpaste (rolled fondant) and flower paste (gum paste). These textured effects can be used on cake boards, cake coverings, drapes, bows and ribbons. Working from the bottom clockwise, the plastic lace is cut from place mats and tablecloths, the dot and floral roller design, then grosgrain followed by silk taffeta and linen. Many other textures are shown in this section of the book.

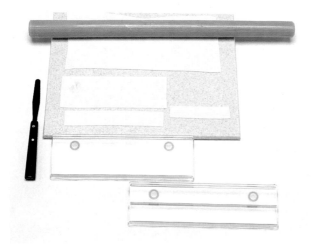

2 For this easy bow, make a 50/50 sugar-paste/flower paste mix, roll out and put through a pasta machine. Roll over using a raw silk roller, then cut out a 5cm (2in) wide strip. Cut this to 14cm (5¹/₂in) long, then cut out 2 x 2.5cm (1in) wide strips. Cut one to 13cm (5in) long, cut the other down a little in width to 2cm (³/₄in) and to 8cm (3in) long. Wrap in cling film (plastic wrap) to prevent drying. (Pasta machines vary; the no. 3 setting was used here.)

3 Fold the larger strip in half for a centre crease. Now pleat the two ends, then the centre. Fold over the two ends to the centre and attach using edible glue. For the tails, pinch, then pleat the paste in the middle. Cut the ends, then fold as shown. Place the smallest strip on a pad and pinch using tweezers. Turn over, brush with glue and place the bow on top. Fold in, trim and secure the ends. Attach the bow to the tail.

4 For a sectional drape, roll out a 50/50 sugarpaste/flower paste mix, then put through a pasta machine. Cut out 3 strips 2.5cm (1in) wide and to the length required. (A strip using a decorative cutter can be used.) Attach first using edible glue, then brush glue on the top edge of a strip. Attach as shown for a petal shape. Stick this on top of the first stage, then repeat. The top strip is formed into a tube shape for a rolled top edge.

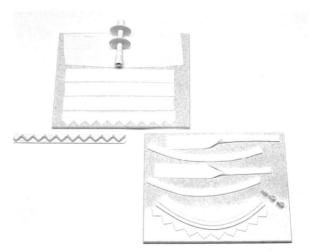

5 Use a clay gun to create many types of rope. Using the large trefoil shape, twist to make a quick rope. A medium plain disc can be used in two different colours and twisted. The braided rope uses small discs in three colours which are then braided. When extruding smaller designs using the clay gun, the clay gun pusher will help to extrude the paste. Use sugarpaste or a mixture of sugarpaste and flower paste for all types of ropes and braids.

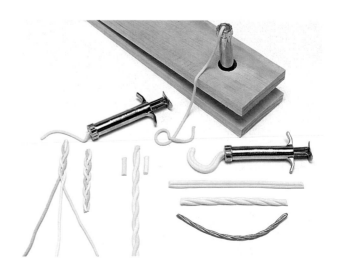

6 For tassels, roll flower paste through the plain roller on a pasta machine. Cut to 8cm (3in) wide and 10cm (4in) long. Dust with cornflour (cornstarch), then put through an angel hair attachment on the machine. Using a modelling tool, pleat in the centre, then fold over and pinch the folded part firmly to hold together. Trim to the desired length using fine scissors. Trim the top a little and dry flat or dry off the rounded edge on a piece of foam.

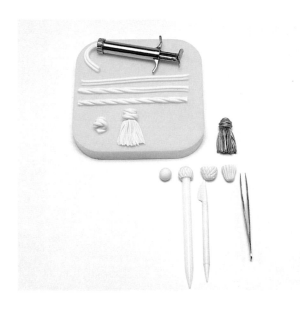

7 For the tassel cord, pass sugarpaste and flower paste mixture through the clay gun using the medium trefoil shape. Twist and attach around the top of the dry tassel base. You can also make other decorative tops for tassels. They can be made in many colours or painted gold by mixing gold powder with lemon extract. (Note: A tassel dried on a curved edge is ideal for the top edge of a cake as it will follow the cake curve. See also page 95 for other tassels.)

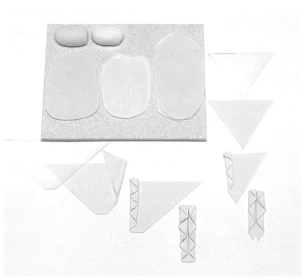

8 Many styles of hangings or jabots can be made. They look effective made in two or three colour combinations. Take equal quantities of sugarpaste and flower paste, then flatten out each colour. Rub a little white vegetable fat (shortening) on to one part, stick the other on top, roll out a little, then pass through a pasta machine. Cut out using a template and fold as shown. This colour technique can also be used for bows and ribbons.

9 This beautiful bow is the one shown on the christening babe cake on pages 92–94. It has a very soft, feminine look. Roll out a 50/50 sugarpaste and flower paste mix. Pass this through a pasta machine, if preferred. Texture the paste using a raw silk rolling pin or roller. Cut out all the bow parts as shown using a template and place in a plastic flap to stop the pieces from drying out before assembly.

10 For a six-tail bow, emboss the edge, turn over and fold in the edge. Turn back over and pleat the edge. For the two bow loops, fold the edges back under, pleat the ends and fold over, sticking with edible glue. Use polyester fibre or foam to support the loops. For the bow centre, fold the edges under, pleat the ends, then bend over the two loops, trimming off excess paste. Assemble the pieces using glue. Support until dry.

11 Here the finished bow has three tails on each side. This can also be made with single or double tails, depending on the size of the cake and how full you want to make it. The patterns for the bow (see page 188) can also be enlarged or reduced to make a larger or smaller bow. Many kinds of bows have been used in decorative ways throughout the book.

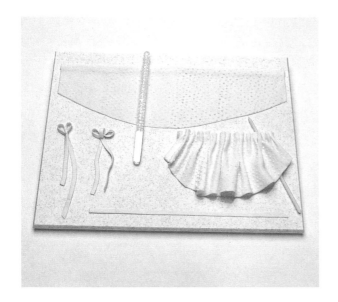

12 Make a 70/30 sugarpaste/flower paste mix (see step 14). Roll out thinly and texture with a pattern stick PS3 (C). Cut a strip 25cm (10in) long and turn one edge under 6mm (¹/₄in). Cut the bottom edge to a curve so that the sides are about 4cm (1¹/₂in) deep and the centre 8cm (3in). Using a small celstick, gather up the top edge, forming soft gathers. The cake used here is 10cm (4in) deep.

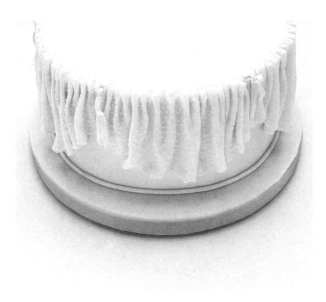

13 Roll out sufficient sugarpaste for the cake top and texture with a dot rolling pin. Lift and place on a cake where the sides have already been covered. Trim and neaten. Mark the edge of the cake into five equal sections. Brush each section with water and carefully lift the freshly gathered paste into place and attach, pressing between the folds with a small celstick while supporting the frill in your hand. Complete by adding bows.

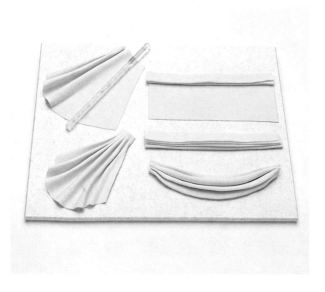

14 Roll out a 70/30 sugarpaste/flower paste (gum paste) mixture and texture with a pattern stick PS8 (C). Cut out a strip 1cm (¹/₂in) deeper than the cake, which is 6cm (2¹/₂in) wide at the top and 16cm (6¹/₂in) at the base. Trim the base to a curve and gather at the top. Cut another piece of paste 2.5cm (1in) longer than the cake sides, and 10cm (4in) deep. Bend at 1cm (¹/₂in) intervals to create four soft folds.

15 Pinch and trim the top of each drape. Brush the top edge with water and press on to the cake corner, allowing the folds to drop naturally. A cotton bud will ease the folds without damage. Grip both ends of the swag between thumb and forefinger and allow the folds to open up. Brush the ends with water and attach on top of the drapes.

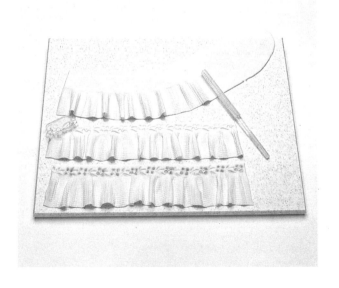

16 Roll out a 70/30 sugarpaste/flower paste mixture to 25cm (10in) by 5cm (2in). Trim one edge straight. Dust the board and paste with cornflour (cornstarch) and placing a pattern stick PS2 (C) 2.5cm (1in) in from the straight edge, roll along the length of the paste, pressing with an index finger. Work backwards and forwards, then straighten the frill to form a fuller gather. Use embosser M1 (C) repeatedly just above the frill and trim the top edge.

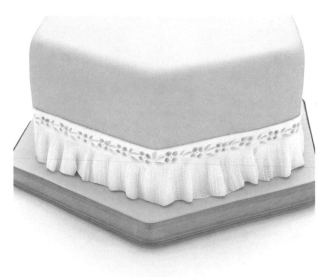

17 To colour the embossed design, carefully cover the frill completely with cling film (plastic wrap) to keep it from drying out. Apply chosen colour of dusting powder using the tip of a fine acrylic paintbrush — take care not to spread the colour about. Brush the top of the edge with water and carefully attach the frill to the cake side. Joins can be cleverly disguised in the folds of the frill.

Flower and bows gift packages cake

When making this style of cake, first make the bows and tags so they will be dry and ready for final assembly. The heart box shown is an accent decoration and can be filled with goodies like candies, truffles and sugared almonds.

HEART CANDY BOX AND GIFT TAG

1 Taking a heart-shaped candy box, cut the lid down to 1cm (1/2in) deep. Brush the top with edible glue, roll out a 50/50 sugarpaste/flower paste mix (rolled fondant/gum paste) and cover the top. Trim and emboss the top as shown. For the box base, roll out the paste, then press the top of the base into the paste. Cut around and stick into the base. Cut out 5cm (2in) wide strips. Attach around the box sides, then attach a strip around the base, trimming to follow the scallop edge. Dry, then pipe a shell around the inside and outside edges using royal icing and a no. 3 tube (tip). Place the lid on to waxed paper and pipe a shell edge. Dry, then dust with super pearl.

2 For the gift tag, roll out flower paste, cut a 9 x 5cm (3¹/₂ x 2in) rectangle, cut to shape as shown and make a hole using a no. 6 piping

Cover the heart box base using equal quantities of sugarpaste and flower paste. Cut the lid down and cover this, embossing the top. Pipe a shell border.

Cake and Decoration

- 3.25kg (7lb) sugarpaste (rolled fondant)
- flower paste (gum paste)
- royal icing
- 64cm (24in) square cake board
- striped gift wrap
- pink and teal green food colourings
- super pearl dusting powder
- 32 x 45cm (12 x 18in) rectangular, 10cm (4in) deep cake
- 20cm (8in) square, 10cm (4in) deep cake
- 15cm (6in) diameter round, 10cm (4in) deep cake
- silver dragees
- silver parcel cord
- silver powder and lemon extract
- gerbera daisy (see pages 134–135)

Special Equipment

- plastic heart candy box (CK)
- embossers (HP)
- nos. 0, 1, 3 and 6 piping tubes (tips)
- size guide (C, ISAC)
- frames 2 mould (C, ISAC)
- diamond patchwork cutter (FMM)
- multiribbon cutter (FMM)
- floral stencil (CC)
- quilting wheel
- stripe stencil (CS)
- floral lace embosser (PC)
- no. 3 strip cutter (JC)
- textured lace set (FMM)

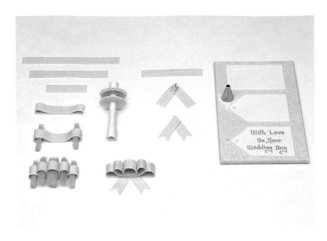

■ Cut out a gift tag and make a hole for the cord. Pipe an inscription. For the bow, cut strips using the multiribbon cutter, then create the bow.

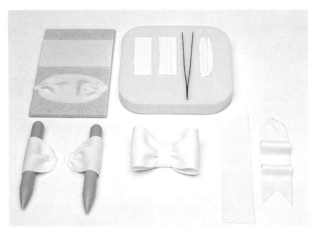

■ Cut out two strips of paste, pleat, fold over and stick on join. Dry, using rolling pins for support. Once dried a little, pinch the centre strip using tweezers, stick around the centre of the loops.

■ Cut out eight diamond shapes, cut off a little from each end, fold over, sticking with glue. Attach four, then another four on top of a disc. For the medallion, push the paste into the frames mould.

tube (tip). Let dry. For the medallion, press a no. 7 ball of paste into the medallion on the frames mould. Dry.

BOWS

3 Roll out the sugarpaste and flower paste mix, cut out two rectangles 13 x 6cm (5 x 2$\frac{1}{2}$in). Pleat both ends, fold over and, using glue, attach at the join. Trim edge. Use foam or a rolling pin to support the loops while drying. Once dried a little, roll out more paste and cut out a strip 9 x 2.5cm (3$\frac{1}{2}$ x 1in). Place on to the soft side of a pad and pinch using tweezers. Turn over and place the two loops on to the strip, attaching with glue. Fold the strip over the back of the loops and trim. Support until dry, then dust with super pearl.

4 For the hatbox bow, roll out sugarpaste and flower paste mix. Cut out 8 diamond shapes and a small round disc. Cut off the edges of the diamonds, fold over and support with foam. Glue at the cut edge. Attach four loops in position, then attach the other four in between. Dry.

5 For the heart box bow, cut strips 1.5cm (2/3in) wide and 6cm (2$\frac{1}{2}$in) long, then 13cm (5in) and 16cm (6$\frac{1}{2}$in) long for the bow and 10cm (4in) long for the tail. Fold over, creating the three loops. Stick together and support with foam. Fold the tail and attach at an angle. Make cuts on the ribbon ends. Stick the bow together and dry.

COVERING THE BOARD AND CAKES

6 Cover the board using striped gift wrap. Colour 1.4kg (3lb) sugarpaste pale pink, roll out and cover the large rectangle cake. Mark the ends using a knife tool and ruler to look like the folded end of a package.

7 Colour 900g (2lb) sugarpaste seafoam using teal green. Roll out to about 25cm (10in) square, place the floral stencil on top and, using a smoother, press into the paste. Dust with super pearl, remove the stencil carefully and cut to a 20cm (8in) square. Place on the cake top, then roll out more paste and cut out four panels, each one the size of the cake side. Attach to the cake sides, then dry for 1–2 hours. Cut out strips 3cm (1¼in) wide and stick around the top edge for the lid. Trim, then position the cake on the large cake.

8 For the round cake, cut a 15cm (6in) circle from white paste. Attach to the top of the cake then, using a pattern, make small dots using a cocktail stick (toothpick) at each intersection. Remove the pattern then, using a ruler and quilting wheel, quilt on the cake top. Press a dragee into each section. Cut a strip longer and wider than the cake side. Using a stripe stencil, stencil super pearl stripes on the paste. Cut to size, roll up gently and unroll around the cake. Roll out sugarpaste and flower paste mix, emboss using lace embossers and cut using the cutter. Attach around the top of the hatbox.

9 To finish the hatbox, pipe a lace design around the top using a no. 0 tube. Dust the bow with super pearl, paint the medallion silver using silver powder and lemon extract, then attach to the centre of the bow. Attach the bow to the cake and place the cake on the square box. Pipe a shell border around the base using a no. 3 tube. For the square box, pipe a lace edge using icing and a no. 0 tube and a shell using a no. 1 tube.

10 For the pink package, roll out white paste made from equal quantities of sugarpaste and flower paste. Emboss using the lace embosser, then cut strips to 4cm (1½in) wide. Dust using super pearl and attach on to the cake, and trim. Cut two 5cm (2in) wide strips. Pleat the ends, dust with super pearl, attach to the cake and create folds. Trim to desired length, using scissors to make a French cut. Attach bow and tails to the cake using royal icing. Thread silver cord through the tag and attach. Write an inscription using silver icing and a no. 1 tube. Pipe a shell border at the base of the large cake using a no. 3 tube.

11 Position the bow using icing, then attach the lid to the base of the heart. Fill with decorations. Make the curly ribbons from two-tone flower paste (see opposite). Arrange in the box. Finish with a gerbera.

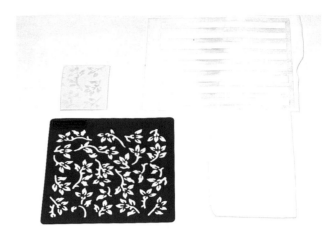

For the top of the middle square package and the sides of the small top package, stencil stripes and a floral design, using super pearl dust to give a satin embossed effect.

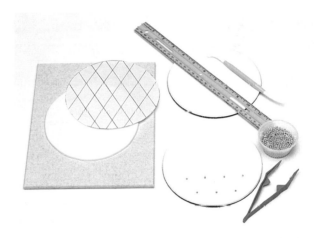

Quilt the top on the round cake with a pattern. Use a cocktail stick to mark each section, then remove the pattern. Using a ruler and quilting wheel, quilt the top, then place silver dragees in each section.

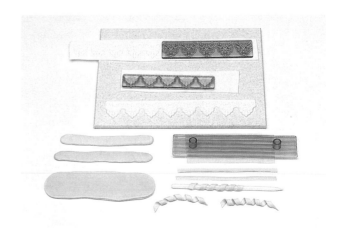

For the top of the hatbox, emboss the paste, then cut and attach a strip around the top. The two-tone ribbons in the heart box are coloured pink and seafoam. The strips are then cut out and curled.

Exotic African animal print

This striking cake, with its drapes and masks, features a number of animal prints using several techniques to achieve the amazing look. The rich colours make this an ideal centrepiece for many different celebrations.

COVERING THE BOARD AND CAKES

1 Cover the cake board with the brown sugarpaste (rolled fondant) and, straight away while the paste is still soft, texture with a crocodile/alligator texture, using items such as a textured box or laminated paper. Leave to dry a little, then paint over with a dark brown/black food colouring using a firm brush to give a texture like crocodile or alligator skin. Leave to dry.

2 Cover the two cakes in cream sugarpaste, stacking the smaller cake on top in an offset design as shown. Taking a little of the sugarpaste that you have left, place into a heavy-duty mixer with a paddle and

Cake and Decoration

- 40cm (16in) round cake board
- 575g (1¹/₄lb) dark brown sugarpaste (rolled fondant)
- dark brown, black and orange paste food colourings
- 32cm (12in) round, 15cm (6in) round x 10cm (4in) deep cakes
- 2kg (4¹/₄lb) cream sugarpaste
- flower paste (gum paste)
- black, chocolate and champagne dusting powders (SF)
- tylose or CMC
- confectioner's glaze
- black royal icing
- cantaloupe lustre dust (ISAC)
- clear alcohol (gin or vodka)
- about 1.5m (5ft) mustard gold ribbon

Special Equipment

- crocodile texture
- firm brush
- nos. 0 and 6 piping tubes (tips)
- mylar stencil plastic (CS)
- electric stencil cutter (optional)
- zebra, cheetah and mask stamps (CS)
- fine strip cutter

Cover the board with brown sugarpaste (rolled fondant). For the crocodile texture, there are several options, such as a textured box or embossed animal-print paper.

Take a stencil sheet, trace a design from fabric or a pattern and place on to a glass sheet. Using a stencil cutter, cut around the marks to create a stencil of an animal print.

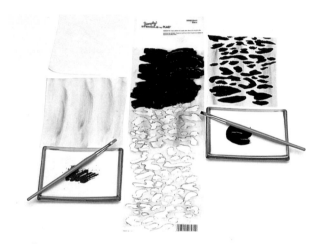

Roll out a cream paste from 50/50 sugarpaste and flower paste. Dust a chocolate stripe, place the stencil on top and press down. Paint over using black colouring. Carefully remove the stencil.

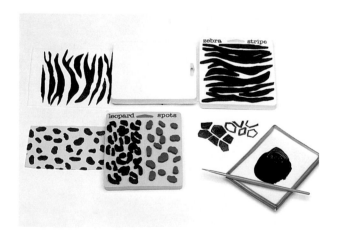

Rubber stamps for craft and wall painting are excellent for cake decorating. Here food colouring is applied to the stamp and then pressed on to the paste.

add a little water until this is the consistency of royal icing. Pipe a shell border using a no. 6 piping tube (tip) around both cakes.

ANIMAL PRINTS

3 Using some mylar stencil sheets, place a sheet on top of a pattern and use a pen to mark the design. Remove and place on to a piece of glass and cut out shapes for stencils using an electric stencil cutter, if available, to give a leopard/cheetah design. Using this technique, any animal print can be made into a stencil.

4 Roll out some paste from equal quantities of sugarpaste and flower paste (gum paste), roll into a strip, then place through a pasta machine. Dust the strips using chocolate brown dusting powder, place the stencil on top and press down using a smoother to stick the stencil to the paste. Then, using black paste colouring, paint over the stencil. Once completed, carefully remove the stencil to show the pattern. Pleat the end and drape on to the cake in the desired shape, folding some of the edges under. (When arranging the drape, be careful as the black design will still be wet).

5 Make the zebra and leopard spots using rubber stamps. Roll out paste made from equal quantities of sugarpaste and flower paste, brush black food colouring all over the stamp and press on to the paste. Carefully remove and repeat as needed. For the leopard spots, use dark brown food colouring. The giraffe markings were painted freehand using brown food colouring. These designs can be made into bows or drapes as shown.

MASKS

6 Take some paste left from covering the cakes and add a little tylose or CMC to make the paste firmer. Roll out not too thinly and brush the mask stamp with dark brown food colouring. Stamp on to the paste, remove carefully and cut around using a modelling knife. Leave to dry.

PORCUPINE QUILLS

7 For the porcupine quills, take various-sized balls of pale cream flower paste, roll into a long thin sausage with points at both ends. Let dry. Dust in stripes using champagne and black/chocolate dusting powder. Place on to paper towel and spray with glaze to give a slight sheen, and set the colour.

FRINGE

8 Cut black flower paste with a fine strip cutter, or angel hair attachment on a pasta machine, and then cut to 2.5cm (1in) sections. When doing this, the cutting will fuse together the ends, making it easier to lift the fringe up in sections. Pipe a line of black royal icing using a no. 0 piping tube along the edge of the paste. Attach the fringe along the edge. Make small beads using orange/brown flower paste. Flatten and brush over with cantaloupe lustre dust mixed with clear alcohol (gin or vodka). Attach these and pipe a lace design consisting of small loops.

FINISHING TOUCHES

9 Once dry, attach the two masks using royal icing. Finally, make small holes in the surface of the cake using the pointed end of a celstick. Gently press the porcupine quills into the holes, preventing them from breaking.

10 Attach the mustard ribbon around the cake.

USEFUL TIPS

• When using rubber stamps, make sure you use a firm and even pressure to create good detail and image.

• If you find the mixture of equal quantities of sugarpaste (rolled fondant) and flower paste (gum paste) dries too quickly, you can use a higher proportion of sugarpaste and less flower paste.

Stamps are used for the African masks. Use strengthened paste, roll out, position the mask stamp and brush the mask with dark brown colouring. Once stamped, cut out the masks and leave to dry.

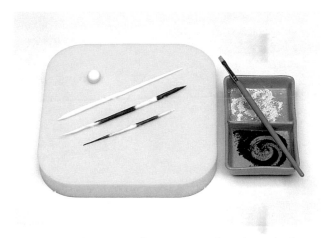

Roll pieces of pale cream flower paste into long shapes for the porcupine quills. Once dry, dust with champagne and chocolate/black colouring. Spray with glaze to give a slight gloss and set the colour.

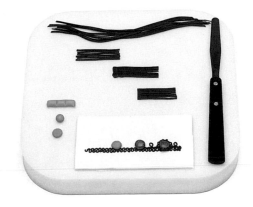

Cut black flower paste into fine strips to make a fringe. Make small beads using orange/brown paste, then paint with cantaloupe lustre dust. Once attached, pipe a lace edge using black royal icing.

Hearts and flowers pillow cake

This attractive heart-shaped cake, edged in box-pleated frills, could be made for many romantic occasions such as an engagement, Valentine's Day or small wedding party. Sugar fabric flowers decorate the pillow.

Cake and Decoration

- 20cm (8in) heart-shaped cake or puff heart-shape cake (W)
- 750g (1lb 9oz) cream sugarpaste (rolled fondant)
- 30cm (12in) board covered in calico (unbleached cotton) fabric
- 2.5ml ($1/2$ teaspoon) tylose powder or CMC
- red and eucalyptus dusting powders
- super pearl lustre dust
- 60g ($2^1/2$oz) red 50/50 sugarpaste/flower paste (gum paste)
- small amount of light green (eucalyptus) 50/50 paste
- little cream royal icing

Special Equipment

- dresden tool
- multiribbon cutter (FMM)
- 6mm ($1/4$in) bead maker
- plain cutting wheel (PME)
- no.1.5 piping tube (tip) (PME)

COVERING THE CAKE AND BOARD

1 If using a normal heart-shaped cake, you will have to sculpt the cake prior to covering to achieve the pillow shape. Cover the cake with the cream sugarpaste (rolled fondant), smoothing around the heart shape. Cover the cake board in cream sugarpaste. When dry, place the cake on the board. Use a dresden tool to press around the base of the cake, making an undercut so that the frill will sit just under the cake.

BOX-PLEATED FRILL

2 Take 175g (6oz) of the remaining cream paste and add the tylose or CMC. Knead into the paste with a little white vegetable fat (shortening). Place into a plastic bag and leave for 1–2 hours to firm up. Remove and roll the paste into a strip. Place through a pasta machine, then cut out using the multiribbon cutter set with one plain

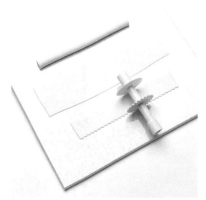

■ Use one plain and one serrated disc when cutting out the paste for the frill around the cake.

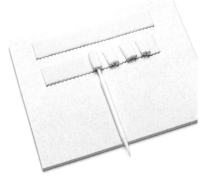

■ Keep the paste in a straight line and work from the serrated edge when forming the pleats.

■ When the paste has been folded over, take care not to press the folded edge or it will become flattened and lose the appearance of softly gathered ribbon.

■ Hold the edges at the base firmly while rolling up the 'ribbon'. The paste needs to be neatly rolled to achieve a rose-like appearance. It is not necessary to 'glue' the paste.

■ Gathering the paste at the point where the edges are attached together creates petals with the soft puffy look of folded ribbon. The red colour will darken as it dries.

and one crimped wheel, using one large and one small spacer on the roller.

3 Place the strips on to a paper towel and carefully dust red dusting powder on to the edge of the frill. Pleat on the soft side of a celpad using a dresden tool to create box pleats. Place the frill around the edge of the cake, attaching it with some edible glue.

PEARLS

4 Roll cream sugarpaste with added CMC (see instructions as for box pleated frill page 64) into a sausage shape, approximately the same depth as the mould. Dust the inside of the 6mm (1/4in) bead-maker mould with cornflour (cornstarch). Open up the mould and place down over the sausage of paste. Squeeze the sides together, trapping the paste inside. Remove the excess paste with a fine palette knife, then opening up the mould just a little, release the paste from both sides with the palette knife, until it is loose enough for the pearls to drop out (do not attempt to pull them free because they will stretch or break). Attach lengths of the pearls around the cake, trimming the ends of each length to fit neatly together.

SUGAR FABRIC FLOWERS

5 Roll out the red paste thinly and cut a strip 3 x 15cm (1 1/4 x 6in) using the plain cutting wheel. If the paste is too thick, the flowers will be bulky. Fold this in half lengthwise, attaching it at the base using a wet brush. Do not press the folded edge.

6 Hold the paste between the thumb and forefinger of each hand and, with the folded edge uppermost, roll the paste tightly a few times.

7 Pinch the paste, then gather it along the base to form petal shapes. Attach these around the centre to form a bud. At all times, try not to press and flatten the folded edge. Trim away any excess paste.

8 For larger flowers, use a longer strip of paste so that extra petals can be added. Trim away excess paste at the back and use egg white to secure if necessary.

Leave the flowers to dry and then shade them with red dusting powder. Lustre powder can be added if desired.

SUGAR FABRIC LEAVES

9 Roll out a strip of pale green paste 2cm (³/4in) wide and cut to a shape that measures 2cm (³/4in) at the top and 3cm (1¹/4in) at the base.

10 Use a cocktail stick (toothpick) to create a fold down the middle, then press down the centre. Turn the paste over and turn in both edges, pinch the top and bottom of the leaves between thumb and forefinger before trimming the excess paste away with fine scissors. Dust with a mixture of eucalyptus and lustre powders.

FINISHING TOUCHES

11 Arrange the flower spray away from the cake so that you are aware of the area that will be covered by the flowers. Pipe spiral curls on to the cake top using cream coloured royal icing and a no. 1.5 piping tube (tip) Allow this icing to dry before transferring the flowers and leaves to the cake top, securing them in place with royal icing.

12 Assemble the rosebuds, open flowers and leaves together. As the flowers and leaves have no stems, they must be placed fairly close together in a tight group to look their best.

USEFUL TIPS

• Flowers and leaves could be arranged in a different-shaped spray and an inscription added to personalise the cake.

• A disc of sugarpaste could be attached to the cake under the centre of the spray to raise the central flowers and give a domed appearance to the arrangement.

• When making pearls, the beadmaker can be dusted with lustre powder colour when a pearlised finish is required.

For buds, use short lengths of paste, but for fuller flowers with extra petals use a longer piece. A wider strip of paste could be used to give deeper petals when making larger flowers.

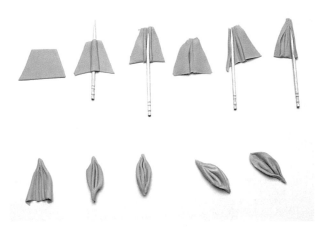

By folding under the outer edges of the leaves, they appear much softer. Make sure to use thinly rolled paste so that the leaves look delicate. Paste that is too thick will produce bulky leaves.

Assemble a selection of buds, flowers and leaves on the cake surface and secure using cream-coloured icing. Be careful not to drop any red powder colour on the cake surface.

Gerbera daisy draped cake

This stylish three-tier wedding cake with its simple drapes and bows is accented with gerbera daisies, eucalyptus and twigs to give a very simple yet elegant effect. Other focal flowers could also be used to create a modern, fresh look.

COVERING THE CAKES AND BOARDS

1 Cover the cakes and boards in white sugarpaste (rolled fondant). Place the large cake on the larger cake board. Stack the two smaller cakes on to the smaller covered board.

DRAPE GUIDE

2 For a drape guide, make a pattern from a strip of parchment paper the length of the large cake. Once cut to size, fold this into four to create a pattern for the cake. Pin around the cake surface and mark the four points where the pattern meets the top of the cake. Remove the pattern and cut one of the sections to use as a template for the drape. If making a fuller or more narrow drape, make this basic pattern wider or more narrow than the original pattern.

Cake and Decoration

- 18cm (7in), 23cm (9in) and 35cm (14in) round cakes
- 28cm (11in) and 45cm (18in) cake boards
- 4kg (9lb) white sugarpaste (rolled fondant)
- 13cm (5in) polystyrene (styrofoam) cake dummy used as separator
- flower paste (gum paste)
- royal icing
- bows and tails (see pages 50–51)
- gerbera daisies, eucalyptus and bear grass (see pages 132–135)
- gold ribbon to trim cake boards

Special Equipment

- raw silk rolling pin or roller (HP)
- no. 5 piping tube (tip)
- wooden satay or cookie sticks
- 5cm (2in) and 2.5cm (1in) strip cutters (JEM)
- multiribbon cutter (FMM)
- 2 posy holders

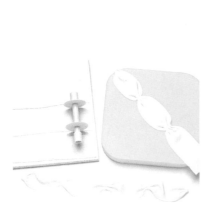

Texture using a raw silk roller and cut a 4cm (1 1/2in) wide strip at each 8cm (3in) point. Pleat to create the effect shown.

Attach around the cake separator, starting at the back and using edible glue to attach. You will need about six sections.

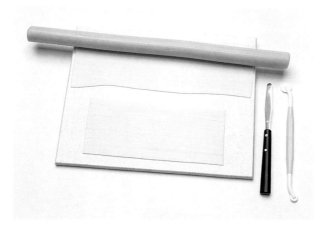

Put some paste through the pasta machine. Remove and texture with a raw silk rolling pin or roller. Cut to shape and size using a template or a ruler.

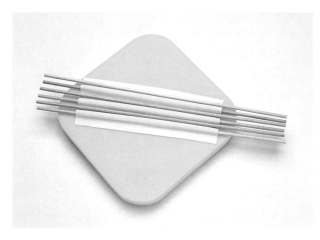

Place wooden satay or cookie sticks on to a pad and lay the paste on top. Position more sticks in between as shown to create folds. More or fewer sticks can be used.

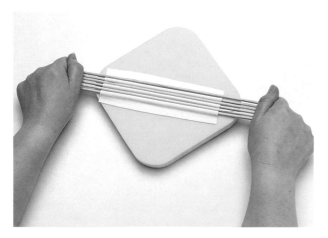

Using your hands, pull the sticks together to obtain the natural pleats in the paste. Working on the pad provides an ideal soft surface for the construction of drapes and bows.

In the cake shown, the pattern is 8cm (3in) wide and approximately 32cm (12in) long.

DECORATING THE SEPARATOR

3 To cover the separator, place a strip of white sugarpaste around the side of the dummy like a bandage. Trim off any excess paste and position on the top of the large cake with the seam at the back. Roll out a mixture of equal quantities of sugarpaste and flower paste (gum paste) and place through a pasta machine, if using. Texture using the raw silk roller. Cut a strip 4cm (1^1/$_2$in) wide.

4 Pleat every 8cm (3in) and place around the separator, sticking with edible glue. Start at the back of the cake where the seam is on the separator and continue until long enough to go around the cake. Approximately six sections will be needed.

5 Pipe a shell border around the cakes using royal icing and a no. 5 piping tube (tip).

DRAPES

6 Roll out more paste in a long rectangle and place through a pasta machine if using. Texture with the raw silk roller and cut to 8cm (3in) and 32cm (12in) long. Working freehand or using the template from the original pattern, place three or four wooden satay or cookie sticks down on to the soft side of the pad. Place the strip of paste on top, then place more sticks in between the original sticks. Using your hands, pull together to create the basic pleating of the paste strip. Remove the sticks.

7 Turn the drape over and fold the top edge over to give a folded top. Pleat the two sides and trim off a little from each end, as this fuses the paste together and helps hold the pleats in place. Brush a little edible glue along the folded edge and bottom edge of the drape. Turn over and position the drape on the cake, trimming off any excess paste at the ends. Continue with the other three drapes to finish off the bottom layer of the cake.

BOWS

8 The bows and tails are made following the instructions on pages 50–51 for the easy bow.

FINISHING TOUCHES

9 To make the drape on the top of the cake, follow the method for a side drape but only pleat one end, then drape down the cake as shown.

10 Arrange two gerberas, eucalyptus and bear grass in a posy holder for the top arrangement. Position a single gerbera, some eucalyptus and bear grass in a posy holder for the smaller arrangement for the side of the cake. Place another drape around the point where the arrangements go into the cake, trying to make it look informal and natural in shape. Trim the cake boards with gold ribbon. Try to keep the finished look simple and balanced, using twigs to give shape and height to the arrangement.

USEFUL TIPS

• You can brush bows, drapes and ribbons with super pearl to make them look like silk fabric, if desired.

• Using cake dummies as separators is a great way to give height to a cake as an alternative to using cake pillars or conventional separators. These can be decorated in many different ways.

• A pasta machine is ideal for rolling out paste of a consistent thickness, making it perfect for drapes, bows and ribbons. Some machines fit on to a Kitchen Aid mixer.

• A separate pasta machine with a handle or an electric motor can be used, attached to your manual pasta machine.

• A pasta machine is also helpful when making flat flower petals for blooms, such as roses and carnations.

• The fact that the pasta machine will give perfectly smooth and even thickness, makes it also ideal for construction work, such as a church or box, so all parts will be neat and equal.

Turn the drape over and fold the top of the drape down to give a folded top edge. Then pleat the two sides and trim off a little paste from each end to fuse the pleated edges, and hold the drape together.

Turn the drape back over and curve the paste to create the draped shape. Brush edible glue on the back along the top and bottom edges, and gently attach on to the cake. Drape to desired shape.

Once on the side of the cake, trim off any excess paste. Continue making the three other drapes to complete the cake. Any bad joins will be covered by bows.

Modelling

In this section, we show several
sugar modelling techniques.
The projects range from a relatively
simple fish shape through to the
more complicated modelling of a
clown figurine. The faces of all the
figurines and the small dove wings
and tail have been made in moulds,
but all the other parts are modelled
by hand. Using the basic principles
shown, and by changing sizes,
bending limbs and turning heads,
other models can be made and
adapted to fit into a wide range
of cake designs.

Modelling techniques: salmon

Materials

- 150g (5oz) 50/50 flower paste/sugarpaste
  (gum paste/rolled fondant) mix
- black, pearlised white, peach and eucalyptus
  dusting powders
- lemon and black paste colours
- 20g (^{3}/4oz) white flower paste
- fine fuse wire or scientific wire

Special Equipment

- pointed tweezers
- 4cm (1^1/2in) ring cutter
- size guide (C)

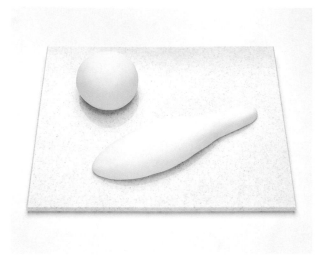

1 The salmon is made from the whole amount of 50/50 flower paste/sugarpaste (gum paste/rolled fondant) mixed together. Working with your fingers, roll the paste to elongate and taper towards one end until about 15cm (6in) in length. Shape, smooth the surface well and flatten slightly. Check for cracks on the surface, and re-roll and shape again if necessary.

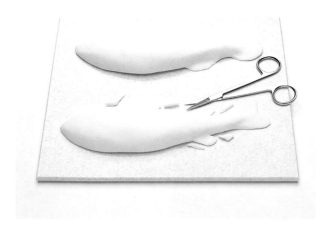

2 To make the fins, start about 5cm (2in) back from the wide end and pinch along the top edge with thumb and forefinger to create the dorsal fin. Repeat the process for a small area along the back, towards the tail and then underneath. Flatten the tail area and gently fan out. Using scissors, trim away small sections of paste to create the fins. Trim the tail to a slight 'V' shape.

3 Picking up the shape, hold carefully so as not to mark the surface. With smooth straight tweezers, pinch the fin areas to create a wavy ridged effect. If necessary, dip the points of the tweezers in cornflour (cornstarch) to prevent the blades sticking to the paste or the points marking the body. Trim again with scissors to improve the shape of the tail and fins.

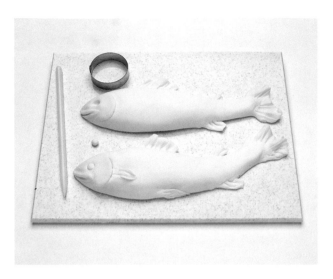

4 Holding the cutter at an angle, press into the paste to form the gill and mark the mouth. Make an eye socket with a large celstick and insert a size 4 ball of paste for the eye. With fine scissors, cut and lift a section of paste near the gill and under the belly. Pinch both with tweezers and smooth underneath. Support the body while drying by placing foam under the head and tail.

5 With a round brush, apply a mixture of black and pearlised powders over the head and back. With a flat brush, apply to the fins and tail. Dust the belly with a peach and pearlised mixture, and add eucalyptus on the side. Add the speckled markings (see caption 6) over the upper part of the head, back and tail. Paint the eye pale lemon, adding a black pupil and white highlight.

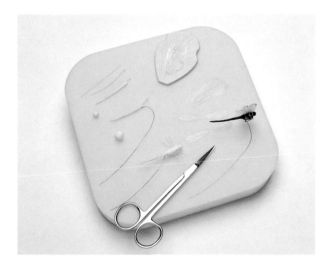

6 To achieve a speckled effect on the salmon, use a firm damp acrylic brush. Dip it into black paste colour, remove the excess on a paper towel, then dab the brush on the upper part of the head, back and tail, allowing the colour to fade down the side. Melted gelatine, when painted over the eye, will give a shiny finish. (See page 77, where the salmon is displayed with a dragonfly.)

7 For the dragonfly, hook the end of a 5cm (2in) piece of 30-gauge wire and partly cover using a size 2 ball of flower paste. Insert the end of a length of fuse wire and curve slightly to form the tail. Shape the body from a size 5 paste ball and insert 3 x 3cm (1¼in) lengths of 30-gauge wire for the legs. Dry before bending using tweezers. Colour and attach gelatine wings. (see step 4 page 76.)

Leaping salmon cake

The cake is suitable for a fishing enthusiast and the design reflects the salmon's characteristic leaping from one level to another. Lifelike bulrushes and an amazing dragonfly adorn the cake.

1 Cut away a cake section at an angle from the top edge to the base. Cover the cake with almond paste and place off-centre on the board.
2 Colour the paste unevenly with navy paste colour and cover both the cake and board with one piece of paste.
3 Mix a small piece of flower paste in matching blue colour and shape two small round 1cm ($1/2$in) deep discs, 2cm ($3/4$in) wide, and attach them to the slope, 10cm (4in) apart. Leave until well dried. These will support the completed salmon away from the cake surface.
4 For dragonfly wings, the gelatine needs to dry very thin. Only flat, finely marked veiners are suitable. Melt 2.5ml ($1/2$ tsp) gelatine, 1.25ml ($1/4$ tsp) sugar and 5ml (1 tsp) water, and drop a little from a teaspoon on to the veiner surface, allowing it to spread thinly. Set until firm as removing too soon will result in the wings curling. Trim, assemble and position stones, bulrushes, leaves and dragonfly.

Cake and Decoration

- 25cm (10in) round cake
- 1kg (2lb) almond paste
- 1.5kg (3lb) sugarpaste (rolled fondant)
- 33cm (13in) round cake board
- navy, brown, black and green paste food colourings
- dark brown, moss green and cream dusting powders
- 30-gauge white and 20-gauge wires
- white floristry tape
- 30g ($1 1/4$oz) mid-green gum paste (flower paste)
- 110cm ($3 1/2$ft), 1cm ($1/2$in) wide dark brown ribbon to trim cake board
- bulrushes
- dragonfly (see page 75)
- wings: 2.5ml ($1/2$ teaspoon) gelatine, 1.25ml ($1/4$ teaspoon) icing (confectioner's) sugar, 5ml (1 teaspoon) water

Special Equipment

- nail brush
- no. 22 veiner (C)
- flat rubber or silicone petal veiner
- size guide (C)
- templates (see page 189)

For the bulrush, build up a wire with floristry tape, cover with flower paste. Texture and dust dark brown. Make stones and leaves, then vein and bend these before drying.

Dove and dovecote

Materials

Dove:

- 100g (3^1/2oz) 50/50 sugarpaste/flower paste (rolled fondant/gum paste)
- polystyrene (styrofoam) block
- 150g (5oz) flower paste
- 20- and 30-gauge white wires
- flesh and black paste food colourings

Dovecote:

- 200g (7oz) white sugarpaste
- 200g (7oz) light green 50/50 paste
- 150g (5oz) mid-grey 50/50 paste
- green and black paste food colourings
- silver powder colour
- clear alcohol (gin or vodka)
- 13cm (5in) diameter round thin cake card

Special Equipment

- size guide (C)
- bird wing moulds (small set) (C)
- serrated knife
- thin card
- dressmaking pins
- plain cutting wheel (PME)
- feather veiner (C)
- acetate or other clear film
- dresden tool
- 9cm (3^1/2in) and 2cm (3/4in) round cutters
- taffeta rolling pin (HP)
- 2.5cm (1in) rose petal cutter
- templates (see page 190)

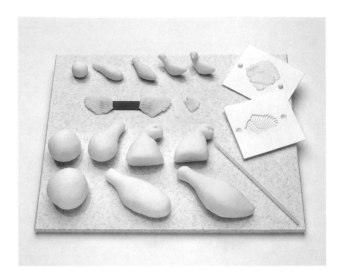

1 For a tiny dove, roll a size 9 ball of 50/50 sugarpaste/flower paste mix to a tapered shape. Form the neck and a tiny beak. Indent and add a size 1 ball of paste for the eye. (The head can be turned while the paste is soft.) For a part dove, shape the head and shoulders from a size 14 ball of paste and texture (a solid body needs size 15).

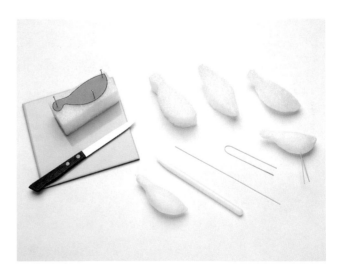

2 Cut a piece of styrofoam 10 x 4cm (4 x 1^1/2in). Pin the dove template to it and cut around, holding the serrated knife at right angles. Trim away towards the head and tail areas to thin at both ends. Keep trimming the edges, then smooth by rubbing all over the surface with a small rolling pin. Bend an 18cm (7in) length of 20-gauge wire and insert from the back to form the legs.

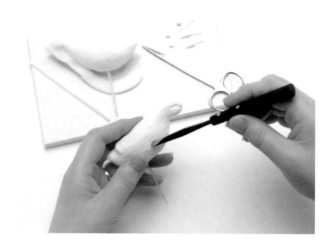

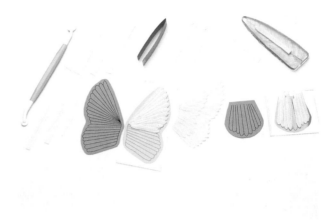

3 Cover the dove shape with 50/50 paste, joining down the centre front. Trim and make a ledge towards the tail area to support dried tail feathers. Indent for the eye socket and add a size 1 ball of paste. Texture over the body and head for downy feathers. A size 2 ball of paste, tapered on to a 2cm (3/4in) piece of 20-gauge wire, forms the beak. Curve slightly and attach to the head.

4 Cut out strips of flower paste, 5mm (1/4in) wide. Shape at one end with a folded piece of thin card. Vein tail feathers and first layer wing feathers on both sides. Others are veined on one side only. Place the drawing under acetate and assemble the wings, securing with glue. Trim feathers. Add a layer of shorter feathers. Join both tail halves in the middle, adding a feather on top.

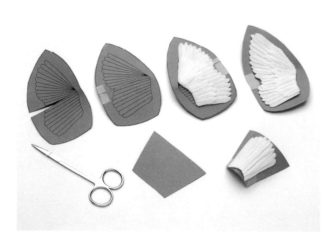

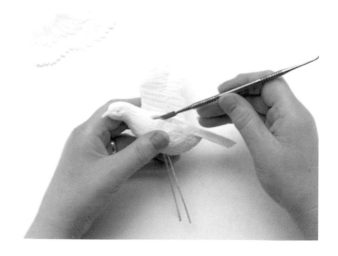

5 Use card to support the assembled wings, while the feathers dry. Make a cut into the card shape and overlap the cut edges, securing with sticky tape, to produce a curve. Place the wings on top of the curves to dry, then remove, turn over and place them inside the curves. Add another layer of shorter feathers to the underside. Support the tail on a curve to dry.

6 Mix flower paste with egg white to make a very sticky glue. Apply a little to the tail support and attach the tail feathers. Use a craft knife to cut a channel in each side of the body. Apply sticky glue and insert the lower edge of the wings. Support while drying. Use 50/50 paste to neaten the front edge of the wings and to fill in any gaps. Blend well and then texture.

7 For toes, roll a size 1 ball of flesh paste to 1.5cm (⁵/₈in) in length on to short pieces of 30-gauge wire. Tape three 'toes' together with ¹/₃ width tape, shorten a fourth toe and secure at the back. Bend the toes before drying and add paste to form the foot. Tape feet to the wires protruding from the body and cover with flesh paste. Blend, shape and texture. Paint the eyes and beak.

8 When attaching the dove (as here on top of the dovecote), position and secure it with the leg wires inserted into the roof. The feet can then be added and the toes can be curved so that they appear to be gripping on to the tiles. Blend extra paste to the feet to complete then, when dry, shade and paint the claws in grey. Extra support may be required if a solid paste body is used.

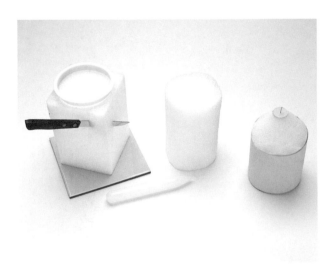

9 Take a 15 x 10 x 10cm (6 x 4 x 4in) block of polystyrene (styrofoam) and, using a 9cm (3¹/₂in) circular cutter as a guide, trim the corners of the block with a serrated knife. Trim the edges, then smooth the surface with a small rolling pin to smooth. Place a strip of thin card 10cm (4in) wide around the form. Secure a 1cm (¹/₂in) disc to the centre top. Cut at an angle to form the roof shape.

10 Place the card template on the side of the styrofoam shape 1cm (¹/₂in) from the base and cut around to create an opening. Cover the total shape with a thin layer of sugarpaste and leave to firm. Roll and cut out grey paste 8 x 10cm (3 x 4in) and cut in from the corners about 3–4cm (1¹/₄–1¹/₂in). Use this to line the cavity in the dovecote. Place on the covered cake card.

11 Texture green sugarpaste with the taffeta pin, then cut a strip 36 x 10cm (14 x 4in). Mark with a ruler to represent wood. Brush the dovecote with water and place the paste around, joining neatly. Cut grey roof tiles using the rose petal cutter. When partly dry, attach in rows on the sloping surface. Make a finial for the top. Mix alcohol with green for the walls and silver for the roof.

12 The dovecote can be made from two 10cm (4in) cakes, 9cm (3in) deep, placed one on top of the other, if preferred. Avoid stretching the 'wood effect' paste. You may find it easier to turn the paste over on to a piece of soft foam and roll around the styrofoam shape. Brush the surface with water, place the covered styrofoam on to it, and roll the two together keeping the paste edge level with the base.

USEFUL TIPS

• When making small doves, the bodies can be hand-modelled, but to achieve realistic wings and tail, it is better to use a mould. Roll out flower paste, not too thinly, and place between the two sides of the mould pieces, interlocking the studs, and then squeeze. Remove the paste and trim away the excess around the edges. Support while drying in a curved shape and then attach to the body.

• For large doves, the bodies can be made from solid paste, but sometimes it is necessary to use a filler so that the finished dove is not too heavy. This method is particularly suitable for the dove cake, where the dovecote and the dove could become a keepsake from the wedding.

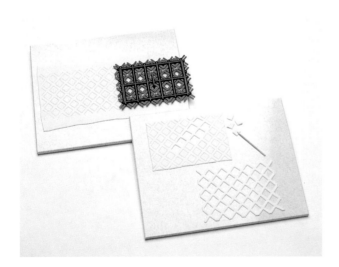

13 The dove and dovecote are used as a top feature for the wedding cake on page 83. A lattice decoration is placed around the side of the base cake – the instructions for this appear in step 2 on page 82. If the paste is too soft when removed from the board, leave for a few minutes to firm up before attaching to the cake.

White dove and clematis cake

This unusual two-tier cake features a gorgeous spray of purple Montana clematis and a dovecote with doves. This beautiful cake would be ideal for a summer garden wedding or celebration.

1 Cover the cakes and board in mint green sugarpaste (rolled fondant). Trim the board with purple ribbon.

2 Roll out white flower paste (gum paste) through a pasta machine if preferred. Rub white fat (shortening) on the board and smooth the paste over. Rub the trellis cutter with white fat and press firmly on to the paste. Remove and continue lining up the cutter. Remove the small squares using a toothpick and trim the trellis to the size. Carefully remove from the board, to avoid stretching. Brush the back with edible glue and attach to the side of the cake, gently pressing with foam.

FINISHING TOUCHES

3 Position the stand and tube at the back of the cake. Tape the smaller sprays together to form a large spray of clematis with a central stem, and position in the posy holder. Arrange the trailing spray around the tube. Position the doves and dovecote on the stand.

Cake and Decoration

- 35cm (14in) oval cake
- 15cm (6in) round cake
- 2.5kg (5¹/₂lb) mint green sugarpaste (rolled fondant)
- 45cm (18in) oval cake board
- purple ribbon to trim cake board
- white flower paste (gum paste)
- white vegetable fat (shortening)
- 15 large and 9 small Montana clematis flowers, 12 small and 16 large buds, and 8 small and 8 large clematis leaf sprays (see pages 128–131)
- doves and dovecote (see pages 78–81)

Special Equipment

- trellis cutter (PC)
- stand and tube for dovecote (C)
- large posy holder

■ Wire a long thin spray and trail around the tube to look like clematis growing up the pole.

■ Tape smaller clematis sprays together to form a large spray with a central stem. Position on the cake.

JUNE TWELVES

Modelling

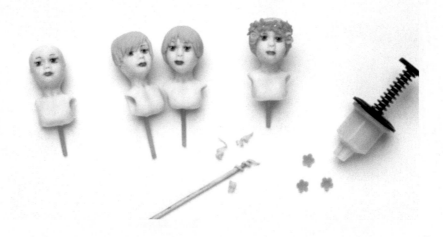

The Holly modelling method provides simple
innovative techniques to make your modelling
easy and enjoyable – a unique introduction to
movement, detail and colour. Although there are
a few modelling tools that you will always find
useful, special equipment is listed with
the projects.

MODELLING TECHNIQUES AND TIPS

To make modelling paste, use a mixture of flower paste (gum paste) and sugarpaste (rolled fondant) in a 2:1 ratio, kneading together well.

For pale skin tones, add a touch of paprika or chestnut paste food colouring. For darker skin tones, add brown to the pale flesh and a tiny touch of green. For oriental skin tones, add tiny touches of brown, green and yellow to the pale flesh colour.

To clothe the figures, use flower paste coloured with food colourings, adding a touch of white vegetable fat (shortening). This will give flexibility and prevent the paste from drying out.

Keep a trace of vegetable fat on your hands when moulding, handling and rolling the paste to prevent sticking.

Use raw dried spaghetti to support the limbs and head. Providing the model is not intended for a small child, bamboo satay sticks or cocktail sticks (toothpicks) may be used as main supports for standing or balancing figures.

Edible glue is used for the seams and securing the clothing. For fixing the body parts together, use modelling paste softened with edible glue.

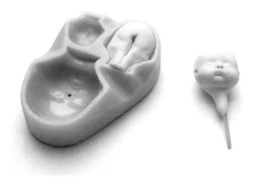

■ **Head:** Press a ball of modelling paste into the mould. Fold the excess paste around the back of the ball. Rock gently to remove. Insert raw, dried spaghetti into the neck.

■ **Faces:** Paint the faces using a no. 00000 brush and food colourings moistened with clear alcohol. Taper the lines using a touch and lift technique.

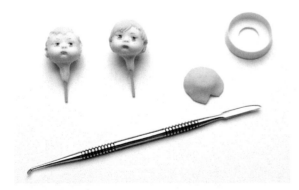

■ **Hair:** Use a mix of softened paste and edible glue, paddled on to the head; or, use a disc of paste, moulded on to the head and textured with curved lines using a ring cutter.

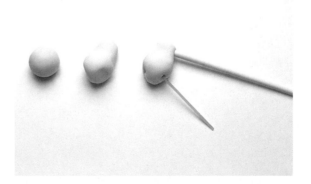

■ **Body:** Roll a ball of paste to a pear-shaped cone. Pinch at the base, indent and lift the shoulder line. Make holes to take the limb supports and head.

PROPORTIONS

While some liberties may be taken with character and comic figures, certain basic proportions need to be considered when modelling figures.

The easy way to determine body proportions is to first measure the length of the head. Use the following as a simple guide:

Small child: Torso – 2 x head length; legs – 2 x head length; arms – 2 x head length.

Woman: Torso – $2^{1}/_{2}$ x head length; legs – 3 x head length; arms – $2^{1}/_{2}$ x head length.

Man: Torso – $2^{3}/_{4}$ x head length; legs – $3^{1}/_{2}$ x head length; arms – $2^{3}/_{4}$ x head length.

In an adult, the hand is generally three-quarters of the head length and the foot approximately a head length.

Legs: Roll the ball to a cone. Roll for the ankle and gently bend the foot over, placing the forefinger behind the ankle and pressing back to establish the heel.

Knee: Place the leg over the forefinger, hold two fingers slightly apart and gently roll in the knee. To define the angle behind the knee, roll between finger and thumb.

Shoes and feet: Mark the sole for shoes. For feet, define the toes under the foot and notch to

■ **Legs:** Roll the ball to a cone. Roll for the ankle and gently bend the foot over. Place the forefinger behind the ankle and press back to establish the heel.

■ **Knee:** Place the leg over the forefinger, hold two fingers slightly apart and gently roll in the knee. To define the angle behind the knee, roll between finger and thumb.

■ **Shoes and feet:** Mark the sole for shoes. For feet, define the toes under the foot and notch to separate the tips. Repeat on the front of the foot. Hollow the instep. Indent the nails.

■ Pinch the inner top thigh to a slight angle. Glue a short length of raw spaghetti into the leg or gently screw a cocktail stick up through the leg.

separate the tips. Repeat on the front of the foot. Hollow the instep. Indent the nails (see below).

Pinch the inner top thigh to a slight angle. Glue a short length of raw spaghetti into the leg or gently screw a cocktail stick up through the leg.

FACE PAINTING

Using a no. 00000 art brush and food colourings moistened with clear alcohol, work on the tip of your brush, using a light touch and lift movement. To achieve a matching left/right image, hold and paint the head upside down.

Paint the eye white. Brush a dark brown line on to the upper lid, flicking up at the end to give the first eyelash. Add one more short curved eyelash. Line the lower lid and the eyebrow.

Outline the iris with dark brown, the top third of the circle disappearing under the top eyelid.

Use grey/blue to fill in the eye colour. Add a dot of black for the pupil.

Outline the top and bottom lip with peachy-pink, then fill in the lip colour.

Add a tiny white dot at the same side of pupil, to indicate light reflection.

To make the head lighter, use a bought paper modelling ball in the centre of the paste.

Arms: Roll a ball into a cone. Roll the wrist and flatten the hand to an oval. Roll the elbow using the knee technique. Emphasise and sharpen the inner angle.

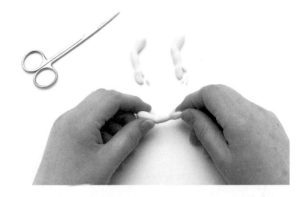

Hands: Cut a small right angle; cut to separate the thumb. Remove a sliver of paste, cut off the tip for the forefinger. Gently smooth the cut edges.

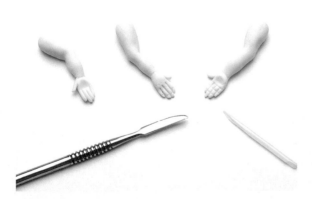

Mark the fingers on the inside of the hand. Notch to define the tips, then repeat on the back. Indent the nails using a toothpick or straw cut to an angle. Define creases with a knife.

Separate a finger and pose the hand in a natural position. Glue a length of spaghetti support into the upper inside of the arm.

Country wedding cake

An easy-to-decorate wedding cake, with country fresh motifs embossed and painted on to a border around the cake sides. This two-tier cake is finished with two charming bridal figures.

DECORATING THE CAKES

1 Brush the cakes with apricot glaze and cover with almond paste. When dry, brush with clear alcohol and cover with the sugarpaste (rolled fondant). Cover the cake boards with sugarpaste, then texture the edges with the silk veining stick. Trim the boards with ribbon.

2 Trellis and fences: For a wood effect, roll white flower paste (gum paste) both sides with the taffeta pin, then cut the pieces with the multiribbon cutter. Brush with mother-of-pearl dusting powder. Leave to dry, then assemble with royal icing.

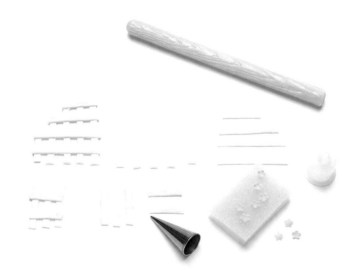

Cut the trellis and fence pieces. Mark 'nails' with the no. 1.5 piping tube (tip). Dry flat, then assemble. Cut 12 flowers for a circlet for the hair.

Cake and Decoration

- 15cm (6in) and 25cm (10in) round cakes
- apricot glaze
- 1.35kg (3lb) almond paste
- clear alcohol (gin or vodka)
- 2.25kg (5lb) sugarpaste (rolled fondant)
- 20cm (8in), 35cm (14in) and 41cm (16in) round cake boards
- 3.1m (10ft 1in) x 1.5cm (5/8in) white ribbon to trim cake board
- flower paste (gum paste): 175g (6oz) white, 115g (4oz) flesh, 25g (1oz) each of yellow, blue and pale grey
- mother-of-pearl dusting powder
- gooseberry green, red, blue, yellow, brown and black food colourings (SF)

Special Equipment

- silk veining stick (HP)
- taffeta rolling pin (HP)
- multiribbon cutter (FMM)
- endless straight frill cutter with fluted blade (OP)
- set nos. 6 and 7 embossers (HP)
- no. 00000 brush
- no. 1.5 piping tube (tip) (PME)
- young adult mould – special edition (HP)
- micro paper modelling ball (12mm) (HP)
- 4cm (1¹/2in) ring cutter
- small ejector cutter (FMM)
- templates (see page 193)
- mini stitch wheel (HP)
- set no. 5 micro embosser (HP)
- ceramic button stick (HP)

Release the head and shoulders by rocking gently in the mould, smooth the mould line. Lift and indent the shoulders. Open the nostrils with a pin or scriber.

Mould a disc of paste on to the head for hair, style and texture. Glue the tiny flowers around the bride's head. Add twisted tendrils of yellow paste.

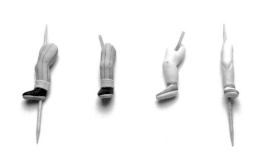

Paint the bride's shoes blue. Paint grey stripes on the groom's trouser legs. Paint the shoes black, add the turn-ups.

3 Place the (35cm) 14in cake board on to the (41cm) 16in board. Lift the cakes on to the boards. Divide the cakes into four. Secure a fence at each of the marked sections.

4 **Border:** Rub a trace of white vegetable fat (shortening) on to a non-stick board and knead a little flower paste into the sugarpaste in a 1:4 ratio. Roll and use the frill cutter to cut one measured section. Emboss the pattern according to length, cover and make three identical sections. Glue around the cake, between the fences. Leave to dry.

5 Paint with the food colourings diluted with alcohol.

BRIDE AND GROOM

6 The figures have been scaled to childlike proportions. Before making the head, body and limbs, refer to the modelling techniques and use the following paste sizes:

Head: 20mm ball; **hair:** 15mm ball

lower torso: 18mm ball; **legs and feet:** 15mm ball

arms: 10mm ball; **hands:** 5mm ball

7 **Head:** Roll the flesh-coloured ball to a cylinder; roll the neck, then place in the mould. Push a length of raw, dried spaghetti into the hole in the micro modelling ball. Press the ball into the paste, folding the excess over the ball and spaghetti. Release from the mould. Smooth the mould line, lift and indent for the shoulders. When dry, paint the face using the no. 00000 brush.

8 **Hair:** Flatten the ball of yellow flower paste to a thick disc. Pinch around the edges, cut a 'V' for the parting. Brush a trace of edible glue on to the head, mould the disc of paste around the head. Carve lines with the ring cutter, working from the crown. Work between these lines with a modelling knife to refine the texturing. To feather the edges, drag the knife down on to the forehead.

9 Using the small ejector cutter, cut 12 tiny blue flowers for the bride's hair.

10 **Legs:** Roll the balls to 3cm (1¼in) cones; pale flesh colour for the bride, the groom pale grey. Follow the modelling techniques on page 86.

11 Insert a cocktail stick through one leg for the main support (left leg of the bride, the right leg of the groom). Mark in the shoe soles. Dry on soft foam.

12 Paint the shoes and the trouser stripes. Add a thin strip of pale grey paste around the ankles of the groom for the trouser turn-ups, 'stitching' around the edge, using the mini stitch wheel.

13 **Lower torso:** Roll the ball of modelling paste (white for the bride, pale grey for the groom) to a 2cm (³/4in) cylinder, form to the template.

14 Glue together the upper and lower torsos, pushing the spaghetti support down through the body.

15 Glue the legs on to the model, pushing the supports into the lower torso. Tip the top of the figures slightly forward. Paint the trouser stripes on to the groom's body, following the lines painted on the legs.

16 **Arms/sleeves:** Roll each ball to 2cm (³/4in) cones (white for the bride, pale grey for the groom). Follow the modelling techniques. Open the narrow sleeve end, ready to accept the hand. Bend the arms and dry on soft foam. (These arms do not have spaghetti supports.)

17 **Hands:** Follow the modelling techniques and glue into the ends of the sleeves.

18 **Dressing the models:** Emboss the skirt with the micro embosser, then pleat the top. Glue around the top edge of the lower torso, joining at the back. Glue the bodice around the upper torso, overlapping at the back. Dust the skirt and bodice with pearl. Add the arms.

19 Glue the shirtfront on to the groom, turning back the collar. Add the waistcoat, dusting both pieces with pearlised dusting powder. Follow with the one-piece coat, turning back the 'stitched' lapels. Add the belt. Glue the arms into position. Press the button stick into five tiny balls of grey paste to make perfectly round buttons; glue on to the groom's coat and belt.

20 Cut more blue flowers to form a circlet around the top of the gate and glue a bouquet into the bride's hand.

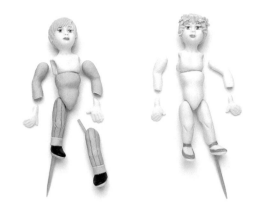

Make and join the upper and lower torsos of the figures, then attach the legs and make the arms/sleeves and hands.

Emboss and pleat the skirt. Dust with pearlised dust, glue just under the upper torso. 'Stitch' the bodice with the mini stitch wheel and glue around the upper torso.

Glue the shirtfront on to the groom and turn back the collar. Add the waistcoat. Brush glue into the armholes and shoulders, and secure the coat.

Christening babe

This pretty pink cake, the babe nestled into the softly draped silk-textured bow, is perfect for any little girl's christening or first birthday. The cake can be covered in blue or lemon sugarpaste, as required.

COVERING THE CAKE

1 Brush the cake with apricot glaze, then cover with almond paste. When dry, brush with clear alcohol and cover with the sugarpaste (rolled fondant). Cover the cake board with sugarpaste and texture with the textured rolling pin. Emboss the cake and board using the embosser. Trim the cake board with decorative pink ribbon.

BABE

2 Before making the head, body and limbs, refer to the modelling techniques on page 85. Use the medium babe head

Cake and Decoration

- 20 x 15cm (8 x 6in) oval cake
- apricot glaze
- 525g (1.25lb) almond paste
- clear alcohol (gin or vodka)
- 800g (1.75lb) pink sugarpaste (rolled fondant)
- 28 x 23cm (11 x 9in) oval cake board
- 1.5m (5ft) x 1.5cm ($^5/8$in) pink ribbon to trim cake board
- bow (see page 53)
- 75g (3oz) pale flesh modelling paste
- 25g (1oz) yellow flower paste (gum paste)
- 25g (1oz) white flower paste
- pink dusting powder (EA)

Special Equipment

- raw silk-textured rolling pin (HP)
- set no. 3 embosser (HP)
- babe head mould, medium size (HP)
- template (see page 192)
- mini stitch wheel (HP)
- ceramic button stick (HP)
- large carnation cutter (SW)
- no. 1.5 piping tube (tip) (PME)
- sugarcraft gun

■ Using the same embosser, impress the edge of the cake board, the base of the cake and the edge of the decorative bow.

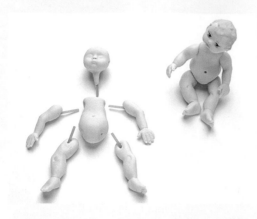

■ Make the head, body and limbs – position the head and limbs on to the body. Secure with modelling paste softened with edible glue. Support until dry.

■ Cut out a nappy from white flower paste and glue on to the babe, adding two tiny buttons. Make the bib using a carnation cutter and attach to the body.

■ Make the toy as described in step 7, then dust with pink dusting powder and slip over the outstretched hand of the babe. Glue carefully into place.

mould. Use the following paste sizes:

Head: 20 mm ball;

Body: 28 mm ball;

Legs and feet: 20 mm balls;

Arms and hands: 17mm balls

FACE PAINTING

3 To paint the facial details, see page 85. For hair, soften yellow, or brown, flower paste (gum paste) with edible glue and paddle on to the head with a small spatula.

ASSEMBLY

4 Glue the limbs and head into position on the body. Support until dry.

5 Cut out the nappy using the template and white flowerpaste. 'Stitch' around the edge of the nappy with the mini stitch wheel, then glue on to the babe. For buttons, press the button stick into two tiny balls of white flower paste. Glue the two buttons on to each side of the nappy.

BIB

6 Using the carnation cutter, cut out the bib. Remove a top section as shown with the wide end of the piping tube (tip). Mark tiny holes with the tip of the piping tube and emboss. Glue the bib into place on the baby. Cut two narrow ribbon strips and attach on to the back of the bib.

TOY

7 Extrude strands of white flower paste through the sugarcraft gun; cut 2 x 2cm (³/4in) lengths and 1 x 3cm (1¹/4in) length. Form the two shorter lengths into rings, thread on to the longer length and join to make a ring. Dust the toy with pink dusting powder and leave to dry on soft foam.

Cake and Decoration

- 15cm (6in) round cake
- apricot glaze
- 450g (1lb) almond paste
- clear alcohol (gin or vodka)
- 450g (1lb) white sugarpaste
  (rolled fondant)
- 20cm (8in) round cake board
- 450g (1lb) yellow sugarpaste
- small amount of yellow royal icing
- 1m (3ft) yellow ribbon 1.5cm (5/8in)
  wide to trim cake board
- 115g (4oz) pale flesh modelling paste
- white, black, red and grey paste food
  colourings for face (SF)
- 50g (2oz) flower paste (gum paste)
  each of orange, white, red, yellow, blue

Special Equipment

- taffeta rolling pin (HP)
- set no. 3 embosser (HP)
- no. 1.5 piping tube (tip) (PME)
- ceramic button stick (HP)
- miniature clown head mould (HP)
- paper modelling ball 12mm (HP)
- clay gun
- templates (see page 194)
- bamboo satay stick
- mini smocking pin (HP)
- mini stitch wheel (HP)
- set no. 1 embosser (HP)
- carnation cutters – small, medium
  and large
- silk veining stick (HP)

Clowning around

*This amazing acrobatic clown is full of character
and movement, daringly balanced on one hand on
a colourful draped and textured drum. A fun model
to make you smile!*

DRUM

1 Brush the cake with apricot glaze and cover with almond
paste. When dry, brush with clear alcohol and cover with the
white sugarpaste (rolled fondant). Cover the cake board with
yellow sugarpaste. Texture with the taffeta rolling pin, then
emboss the edge with the no. 3 embosser.

2 Lift the cake on to the board. Using the no. 1.5 tube (tip)
and yellow royal icing, pipe a snail's trail around the base of
the cake.

3 Roll the yellow sugarpaste (rolled fondant) to a circle,

Pipe the tassels on to the edge of the textured drape, following the
sequence shown. Finish with buttons using the ceramic button stick.

Paint the face, extrude the hair, then using a cocktail stick to pick up small sections of hair. Fix on to the head and separate the strands.

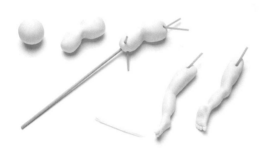

Model the body (see template on page 194), inserting the temporary supports as shown. Model the legs, glue spaghetti supports into top inside thigh.

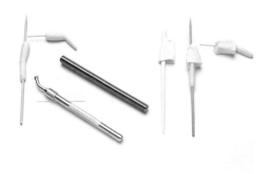

Make the arms, then cut and seam the sleeves. Pleat the top edge then glue them on to the arm, completely enclosing the arm in the sleeve.

texture with the taffeta pin and cut to a 35cm (14in) circle. Drape over the cake. When just beginning to set, trim the edge just clear of the board.

4 Pipe a snail's trail around the edge of the drape. Pipe tassels from the edge of the drape, down to the board. Make buttons for the tassels, pressing the button stick gently into small balls of paste. Trim the cake board with ribbon.

CLOWN

5 Before making the head, body and limbs, refer to the modelling techniques on page 85 and use the following paste sizes. Allow the work to dry between stages.
Head: 18mm ball; **body:** 30mm ball; **legs:** 25mm balls; **arms:** 15mm balls; **gloves:** 15mm balls.

Stage 1

6 Head: Press a paper modelling ball into the paste in the mould, release and open the mouth using a cocktail stick.

7 Painting: When dry, paint white around the mouth, the eyes and half ovals over the eyes. Outline in black. Paint the eyes following the modelling techniques. Outline the nose and mouth, then paint red.

8 Hair: Soften a little orange flower paste (gum paste) with edible glue and apply to half the head. Extrude 1cm (1/2in) lengths of coloured paste from the clay gun, then glue the extruded hair into place. When dry, repeat to complete the head.

9 Body: Roll the ball to a 5cm (2in) cone, form to the clown template. Insert a greased satay stick through the body, entering at the right-hand top shoulder. Push a piece of greased raw dried spaghetti into the left-hand shoulder. Make a hole diagonally in the back of the neck edge, ready to take the head after dressing. Push a length of greased spaghetti into the hole. Insert greased spaghetti into the lower torso for leg supports. (All supports are temporary.)

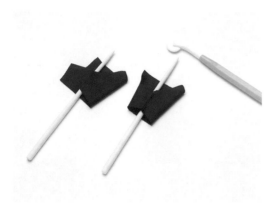

Cut the trousers and make the leg seam. Slip from the ceramic tool, over the leg and on to the body of the clown, overlapping the centre bodyline.

Add the trouser waistband and turn-ups, rib-roll and make the vest, enclosing both side seams. Emboss and stitch the waistcoat. Glue into place.

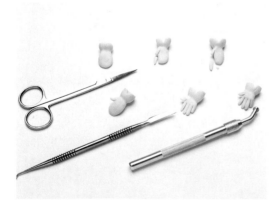

Open the wide end of the cone and take out a 'V' shape. Follow the modelling techniques for the hands. Remember to make one right and one left.

10 Legs and feet: Roll the balls to 7cm (2³/₄in) cones, and follow the modelling techniques. Glue spaghetti into the inner thigh, leaving 2cm (³/₄in) protruding at the top. Dry on soft foam.

11 Arms (no hands): Roll to 5cm (2in) cones, and follow the modelling techniques. Gently screw a greased bamboo satay stick up through the centre of one arm (main support). Make the second arm, and glue in spaghetti supports. Dry the arms on soft foam.

12 Rib-roll the sleeves using the miniature smocking pin, 'stitch' with the wheel, then pinch three pleats into the top. Secure the seam, slip on to the top of the arm pushing the supports through the paste. Glue, completely enclosing the top of the arm.

13 When the legs are thoroughly dry, glue on to the body.

Stage 2

14 Trousers: Roll the red paste thinly, make the leg seam. Tip the trouser leg from the ceramic stick over the leg, on to the lower torso. Glue into place, overlapping the centre bodyline to ensure a safe and tidy seam. Reverse the pattern piece for the second side. Glue the front and back seams. Ease the front of the trousers away from the body.

Stage 3

15 Waistband and turn-ups: Stitch one edge, then glue on to the trousers.

16 Vest: Rib-roll, then make the side seams. Brush glue on to the clown's shoulders and around the armholes. Remove the spaghetti arm support. Insert the body into the vest, pushing the satay support through the paste, ease around the shoulders. Remove the satay stick and, using a little softened paste, secure the support arm/sleeve into place. Fix the second arm/sleeve.

17 Waistcoat: Stitch and emboss with set no. 1 embosser. Brush edible glue on to the shoulders and side seams of the shirt. Position the back of the waistcoat; bring the front over the shoulders to overlap and firmly secure the side seams.

18 Gloves: Roll into 2.5cm (1in) tapered cones, open the wide end of the cone for the gauntlet, taking out a 'V' shape on the edge. Follow the techniques for the hands, stitching along the fingers. Glue on to the ends of the arms.

19 Position the clown on the cake.

20 Collar: Cut one large, one medium and one small carnation shape. Dust with mother of pearl, then frill around the edges using the silk veining stick. Glue the large frill on to the shoulders, followed by the medium and small ones. Glue the head through the frills and into the body. Support until dry.

21 Tie and pocket: Drop tiny balls of red, blue and yellow paste on to the rolled white paste. Roll over once. Cut the two tie pieces, stitch, pleat and add the knot. Glue under the frill. For the pocket, stitch the top edge and glue into place.

22 Buttons: Drop tiny balls of paste on to the board, and gently press in the ceramic button stick. Glue on to the waistcoat, pocket and waistband.

PROFESSIONAL TIPS

• To allow the paste to drape naturally, dress the clown while he is upside down. The clothes should be loose, following the movement of the clown.

• For neat seams, first make the clothing off the model, then carefully slide the seamed garment on to the model.

• To ensure the paste does not adhere to the body and legs, dust the inside of the paste with cornflour (cornstarch) before making the seam.

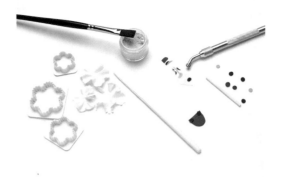

Frill the collars with the silk veining stick, make a spotted tie, adding the second shape for the knot. Finish with a pocket and buttons.

Attach the collar frills, one at a time, to the clown. The clown's head is then attached to the body through the frills. Support the head until dry.

Authentic-looking buttons are made by impressing a ceramic button stick into tiny balls of paste. These buttons add a finishing touch to models.

Needlework in sugar

In this section, we have used many needlework and embroidery techniques and transformed them into sugarcraft ones. We have included patchwork, quilting, cut-out work, broderie Anglaise, cross stitch and all kinds of embroidery stitching. The sewing basket and miniature wedding cake show how to use some of the ideas. To perfect these techniques, practise first, especially the various embroidery stitches. The sewing basket cake contains many needlework items, but just one or two of these could be used on a much simpler design suitable for a needlework enthusiast's celebration cake.

Needlework techniques

Patchwork is made up of many designs, and different colour combinations can be incorporated. Other shaped cutters can be used to cut out this type of patchwork.

The design below has been worked in Christmas colours, but other colour combinations create different effects. Equal quantities of sugarpaste (rolled fondant) and flower paste (gum paste) are the mediums for making patchwork. While working, keep the pieces in a plastic flap to prevent drying out before finishing and for pressing on the design.

After you create each design, cut out the diamond or other shapes for the patchwork. A square patchwork is also shown using square cutters.

Ideas for patchwork can be found in books or on the internet. You will get ideas on colour combinations and formations of shapes to create in paste. Various template shapes can be found in craft stores: these shapes can be cut around instead of using a cutter.

For inspiration, look at antique quilts found in stores, for ideas on colours and shapes used in combination with each other.

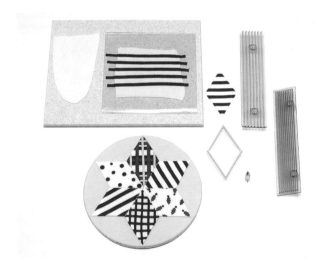

1 For the patchwork design, roll out a white 50/50 sugarpaste/flower paste (rolled fondant/gum paste) mix and place in a plastic flap. Cut out contrasting colour strips and place at intervals on the paste. Gently press over the top of the plastic. Remove the top sheet and cut out a diamond shape. For the plaid, use two different-sized strip cutters and three colours of paste. For dots, roll small balls of paste, place on the base paste and press under plastic. For the holly design, place paste holly leaves on the base paste and press small balls of red paste on top for berries.

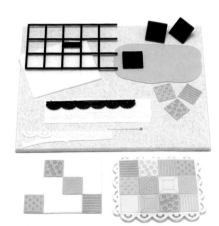

2 To make patchwork using square cutters, mark the grid design on to the cake or paste. Roll out flower paste, rub a little white vegetable fat (shortening) on to the board, and rub a little fat on to the cutter, then press on to the paste. Remove the design square and stick on to the grid using edible glue. The lace edge is made in the same way as the squares. Once cut out, remove the piece using a pin and attach around the quilt.

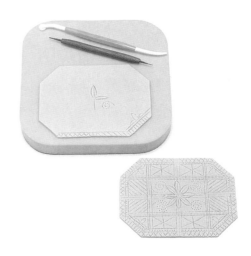

3 Inspired by antique matelassé quilted fabric, this is a very fine quilted design of intricate pattern. It can be worked on to a plaque, the top of a cake or a cake board. Use a small quilting wheel for the straight lines and the small end of a stylus ball tool to mark the curved designs as shown. It is best to plan a basic pattern on paper first before you start work as the paste will dry fairly quickly.

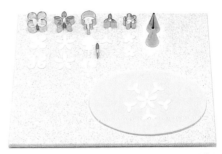

4 Cut-out work can be created to give the effect of a lace doily. Roll out flower paste, then cut out shapes using various cutters. Flower cutters, including hydrangea, stephanotis, nasturtium, bittersweet and blossom, are used here. Cut holes using no. 3 or 5 piping tube (tip) ends. Once attached with glue, dry a little then outline and join up the sections using a no. 0 or 00 tube with white royal icing, with a moist paintbrush to neaten joins.

5 This intricate design is adapted from battenberg lace. Like the cut-out work, this lace is made using flower paste. The yellow cutters are used to make the main design and then no. 2 strips from a strip cutter are cut out to fill in between the design. Where pieces join, use a little soft royal icing and a paintbrush to fill in between. Pipe lace edge and lines using a no. 0 piping tube.

6 For broderie anglaise, various strip cutters and additional cutters are used. Cut plain holes using a no. 3 or 5 piping tube. Once completed, pipe around the cut-out design and edge using a no. 0 or 00 piping tube. Here, the designs are first embossed, then a dresden tool is pressed into the design to hollow out. Outline with royal icing. Broderie anglaise looks most effective with a contrasting colour underneath.

7 Hem stitch and satin stitch are created using a no. 00 piping tube. The hem stitch can be used to attach sections together and even used on broderie anglaise and cut-out work. The satin stitch is a good technique for lettering and can be adapted to monograms for the top and sides of cakes.

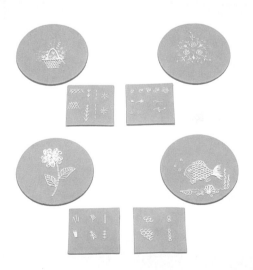

8 Shown here are four plaques, each using different freehand stitch techniques. These are all piped in a no. 0 or 00 piping tube (tip). Working from bottom left-hand side clockwise, the flower motif uses long and short stitch, fishbone stitch and couching. The flower basket uses herringbone, fern, running and star stitch. A floral freehand design is created with freehand embroidery techniques. The fish uses feather and chain stitches.

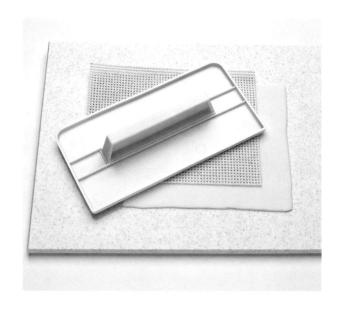

CROSS STITCH

1 First, prepare a 'canvas' for the cross stitch to be worked on, either by marking a freshly covered cake top or a still-soft sugarpaste plaque with a suitable grid. Make this by pressing on an embroidery canvas or a grid marker with a cake smoother to transfer the design into the soft paste. Remove the canvas carefully. An area approximately 14 x 10cm (5^{1}/$_{2}$ x 4in) is required.

2 Transfer the chart on page 192 on to squared paper. (This helps to understand the design and, when coloured with pens or crayons, is easier to follow.) Measure 3cm (1^{1}/$_{4}$in) from the top and 4cm (1^{1}/$_{2}$in) from the left-hand side, and pipe four yellow crosses into a square using a no. 0 piping tube (tip). Following the chart, count and pipe crosses in the correct position, starting with a mid-pinky mauve and then a darker shade of royal icing.

3 Make up three tones of green royal icing. With the darkest shade of green icing and no. 0 piping tube, pipe a line for the stem and complete the outside portion of the lower leaf. The upper leaf is worked in mid-green and both centre lines in the lightest green. Use a damp brush to neaten any spikes left at take-off points.

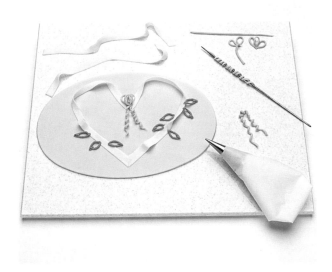

RIBBON HEART

1 Thinly roll out a mix of 50/50 white sugarpaste/flower paste and cut two strips 15cm (6in) x 6mm (1/4in). Place in a heart shape and join neatly. Using a no.1 tube and softened green sugarpaste, pipe leaf shapes, with a securing stitch at the top. Neaten. Roll a size 3 ball of paste into a thin strip and make three ribbon loops. Spiral a strip around a needle tool. Attach loops and twists to the heart shape.

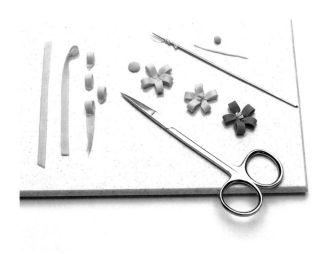

2 Roll out 50/50 pink and violet paste very thinly and cut into strips 4mm (1/6in) wide. Bend and attach with edible glue, making small loops. Secure and cut. Flatten a size 2 ball of paste and attach five loops to this to form a flower. Roll out a yellow size 1 ball of paste, wind round a needle tool and remove. Form into a knot for the flower centre.

3 The finished flowers can be attached when the piped leaves are dry. Many different flower types can be formed with individual ribbon petals made in this way. Equal quantities of sugarpaste and flower paste are used to make this heart decoration less fragile.

RIBBON EMBROIDERY HAT

1 For the embroidery hat, cut 50/50 yellow sugarpaste and flower paste into strips 10cm (4in) x 6mm (¼in). Place about 10 strips side by side. Weave alternate strips until enough area has been worked to be able to cut out with a 6.5cm (2½in) circular cutter. Cut a second arc to fit the template (see page 189). Cut strips of paste 3–4cm (1¼–1½in) long, overlap and secure to form the brim. Trim neatly to fit to the crown.

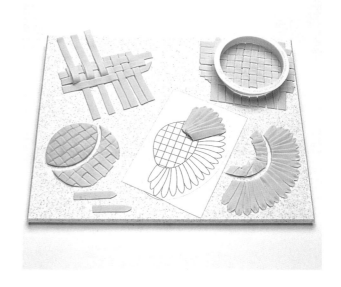

2 Attach the hat to a cake top or plaque, placing a flattened size 10 ball of paste under the crown to pad. For the hat band, roll a size 6 ball of lilac 50/50 paste into a long strip and pinch at intervals with tweezers. Attach in position at the join. Referring to the previous project, make ribbon petals and add leaves and centres. Triangular leaf shapes are cut from a 1.5cm (⅝in) strip of paste.

3 Place the ribbon petals on to the embroidery hat, side on, so that the loops show. Add the flower centres and leaves, and then finish with narrow loops and tails. This pretty design could be varied using different colours and flowers. The hat makes a delightful cake decoration.

Sewing basket

This novelty cake is wonderful for anyone who likes needlecraft; a knitting or patchwork theme could be made by adding different items for each hobby. The cake top could be made as a plaque to remove and keep as a memento.

Cake and Decoration

- 900g (2lb) cream/brown sugarpaste (rolled fondant)
- 23 x 34cm (9 x 13in) cake
- 32 x 42cm (12 x 16in) cake board covered with pink foil
- sugarpaste
- flower paste (gum paste)
- various food colourings
- super pearl lustre dust
- silver powder mixed with lemon extract
- gold food colouring

Special Equipment

- basket-weave roller (PME) or basket-weave embosser (PC)
- raw silk roller (HP)
- clay gun (ISAC)
- heart mould (CS)
- geometric set (FMM)
- scissor cutter, embroidery grid and doily B cutter (PC)
- size guide (C)
- grosgrain roller (ISAC)
- nos. 0, 00 and 9 piping tubes (tips)
- edible food pens
- push moulds (ISAC, C)
- multiribbon cutter (FMM)
- silicone moulds (CK)
- square cutters

COVERING THE CAKE

1 Colour 900g (2lb) sugarpaste (rolled fondant) with cream and brown food colourings for a basket colour. Roll into a sausage, then into a rectangle. Using the basket-weave roller or embosser, texture the paste. Cut to the size of each side of the cake and then attach, covering all four sides.

2 Roll out pink paste made from equal quantities of sugarpaste and flower paste (gum paste). Roll this thinly, then texture using the raw silk roller. Dust super pearl over the surface, then lay on top of the cake and ruche up to look like fabric. Trim off excess paste.

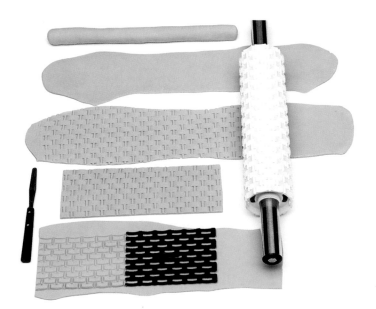

Roll out cream/brown sugarpaste (rolled fondant). Texture using a basket-weave roller or embosser and cut to the size of each side of the cake. Carefully attach to the cake sides. When doing this make the strip longer and wider than needed.

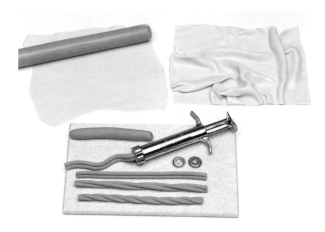

For the pink fabric basket top, roll out 50/50 sugarpaste and flower paste very thinly. Texture using a silk roller, dust with super pearl and attach to the cake. Use a clay gun for the rope.

Press paste into a heart mould. Roll out 50/50 sugarpaste and flower paste, then texture using a grid embosser. Cover the heart. Press doily cutter on to the paste, trim off the lace edge and attach.

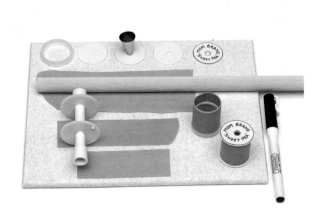

Cut out cream discs and make holes using a piping tube. Use edible pens for writing. Texture pink paste with a grosgrain roller, cut a strip and wrap around a small pot. Once dry, assemble reels.

3 Roll basket-coloured covering paste into a long sausage the size of the barrel of the sugarcraft gun. Cut into sections the length of the gun and place into a plastic bag to stop drying. Place one length into the barrel and extrude paste using the large trefoil shape. When the plunger is about 2.5cm (1in) from the end, pull out, refill and continue. This will provide a double length piece of paste. Twist to create a rope and attach around the top of the cake, creating a mitre at each corner. Any joins or imperfect areas can be covered with ribbons or lace.

HEART PIN CUSHION

4 Fill the heart mould with sugarpaste, and remove. Roll out 50/50 sugarpaste and flower paste, and texture using the embroidery grid embosser. Brush edible glue over the heart shape and cover with the textured paste. Do this very carefully so as not to distort the design. Trim off excess paste and smooth around the edge. Roll out some flower paste, lay on to a board rubbed with white vegetable fat (shortening), and press doily B cutter on to the paste. Remove and trim off excess paste to leave just the frill. Attach around the edge of the heart shape using edible glue. Press in with the back of the dresden tool to create a scalloped edge. Make a small hole in the pin cushion for the needle.

SCISSORS, THIMBLE AND NEEDLES

5 Make these items using white flower paste. For scissors, roll out paste on a little shortening. Press the scissor cutter on to the paste. Carefully remove excess paste, lift the scissors off the board, and place on to the soft side of a celpad. Reshape if necessary and leave open or closed. Make the needle from a no. 2 ball of paste. Roll into a needle shape 4cm (1¹/2in) in length. Use a modelling knife to make the eye in the top. Some needles can be cut in half to use in the pin cushion. Make the thimble in a mould (see page 14 on making moulds). Once dry, paint using silver powder mixed with lemon extract.

REELS/SPOOLS

6 Roll out cream flower paste and cut out using a round 3cm (1¼in) cutter. Cut a hole in the centre of the disc using a no. 9 piping tube (tip). For the thread, take colour of your choice made from 50/50 sugarpaste and flower paste. Roll out into a strip and roll the grosgrain roller over. Cut to a strip 3.5cm (1⅝in) wide – this is two large spacers on the roller – then cut to about 9.5cm (3¾in) long. Wrap loosely around a small powder container to dry, trimming off excess but leaving a slight overlap for strength. Dry for about 1 hour, then remove to dry the inside. Use food colour pens to write on the discs. Assemble using royal icing.

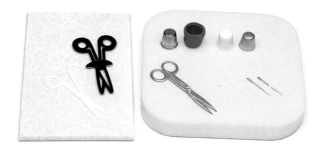

Press a scissor cutter on to flower paste. When dry, paint with silver. Make the thimble from a mould and the needle from a no. 2 ball of paste rolled into shape. Once dry, paint both silver.

BUTTONS

7 The buttons are all made from flower paste. For the basic buttons, cut out using various piping tubes and small cutters. The small holes are made using the fine ends of tubes. Paint shirt buttons to look like mother of-pearl using super pearl dust mixed with clear alcohol, then paint a little brown on the edge. Suitable real buttons were used to make moulds from silicone plastique. Some of these were painted gold or brown to look like brass or wood. Push moulds were also used for silk French knot buttons, and small flowers and pansies looking like decorative buttons. Cut out the buckle using two different-sized square cutters. Form the centre from rolled paste. Once dry, paint gold.

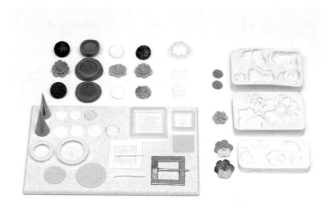

Mould the assorted buttons from push moulds, silicone plastique moulds, and using cutters and piping tubes. Make the buckle using square cutters. These are made in colours to match the basket.

FINISHING TOUCHES

8 Make the ribbons using rollers, lace embossers and ribbon embossers. Drape into the basket while soft.

9 Start arranging items into the basket. Attach the dry items using royal icing for support. Pipe a dot design on to the pin cushion to look like cross stitch, and a lace edging piped with a no. 0 tube. Once the main items are in place, fill with ribbons, buttons and lace motifs. These items do not all need to be attached with icing as the rope edge will hold them. Place the needles in position and, using a no. 00 tube, pipe the threads.

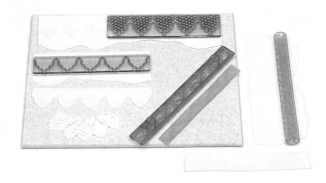

Lace embossers, ribbon embossers and floral drape rollers are used for making different ribbons. Drape and position the various ribbons into the basket while still soft.

Mini wedding cake

These delightful mini cakes can be made for each guest at a wedding, or for a select few at the the top table. They can be single- or two-tier cakes and decorated more simply or intricately.

COVERING AND ASSEMBLING THE CAKES

1 Cover the three cakes in lemon sugarpaste (rolled fondant). When covered, place a larger-sized cookie cutter over each cake to cut off excess paste. Cover the 8cm (3in) board in lemon sugarpaste. Choose either a 14cm (5½in) mirror base or the cake board, covered. Attach the small cake to the small board and the large cake to the mirror or larger board.

2 Make a 10cm (4in) and 8cm (3in) circular pattern out of paper for the drape and pillar positions. Fold the 10cm (4in) circle into four sections. Place on top of the large cake and mark the four points at the folds on the edge of the cake for the drape position.

3 Attach the middle cake to the large cake. Place the other pattern on top and mark into three sections, with the mark 1.5cm (⅝in) from

Cake and Decoration

- 10cm (4in), 8cm (3in) and 5cm (2in) round cakes
- 225g (8oz) lemon sugarpaste (rolled fondant)
- lemon yellow food colouring
- 8cm (3in) round cake board
- 14cm (5½in) bevel-edge round mirror or cake board
- flower paste (gum paste)
- royal icing
- tylose or CMC
- super pearl dusting powder

Special Equipment

- round cookie cutters (optional)
- 3 wooden skewers
- nos. 807 and 805 piping tubes (tips) (AT)
- nos. 1 and 7 piping tubes (tips)
- grosgrain roller (ISAC)
- multiribbon cutter (FMM)
- drinking straws
- small bell mould (FMM)
- size guide (C, ISAC)
- mini drape and bow mould (SC)
- lace edge cutter from patchwork squares set (PC)
- mini daisy cutter (C, ISAC)

Cover the three cakes and small board using sugarpaste (rolled fondant). You can use a cookie cutter larger than the cake as an easy way to remove the excess paste.

Position the cakes on a mirror base as on the previous page, or on a covered board as shown in this photograph. Make a pattern to mark the position of the drapes and pillars.

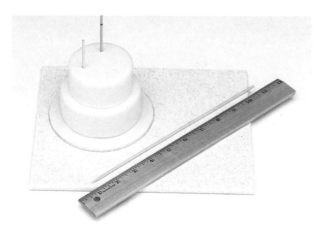

To support the cake, push wooden skewers into the bottom two tiers until they reach the cake board at the base. Mark and cut to 4cm (1¹/2in) above the cake.

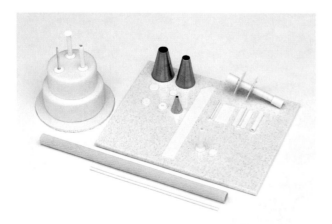

Cut out discs from 50/50 paste using piping tubes, then stick together. Make a hole in the centre, roll out some more paste, texture, and cut a strip. Wrap around a straw for a cake pillar.

the edge of the circle. Mark these three points for the position of the pillars.

4 Push wooden skewers into the three marks on top of the cake all the way through until they touch the cake board at the base. Mark 4cm (1¹/2in) from the cake on the skewer and cut off excess skewer.

5 Roll out 50/50 sugarpaste/flower paste (gum paste) and cut out six no. 805 tube (tip) discs and three no. 807 tube discs. Stick the smaller discs on top of larger ones for the base of the three pillars using edible glue. Make a hole through the centre of the discs using the end of the no. 7 piping tube. Slide these over the skewer and down to the top of the cake.

6 Roll out some more paste, texture using the grosgrain roller, then cut strips 2cm (³/4in) wide. Cut the strips to 4cm (1¹/2in) long. Turn over and brush with edible glue then, taking a 4cm (1¹/2in) section of drinking straw, wrap the paste around to cover the straw. Pipe a little royal icing at the base of the discs and then slide the covered straws over the wooden skewer. Use a little more royal icing on the top of the skewer and place the three remaining discs cut from the no. 805 tube on top.

CAKE-TOP DECORATION

7 Taking a little of the leftover covering paste, add some tylose or CMC to make it a little firmer. Roll and cut out a 2.5cm (1in) disc and a disc from the wide end of a piping tube. Stick together using edible glue and press the small bell mould into the centre to make an indentation. Make a pad of paste, dust with cornflour (cornstarch) and press into the bell mould. Use the rounded end of the medium pin to hollow out. Trim excess paste and leave for about 20 minutes. Turn out and dry the outside. Stick on the base using royal icing. Decorate using a no. 1 piping tube and royal icing.

DRAPES AND BOWS

8 Roll a no. 8 ball of 50/50 sugarpaste and flower paste and make into a sausage the length of the drape

with pointed ends. Dust with cornflour and press into the drape mould using a dresden tool to create details. Remove and dust with super pearl dust. Attach to the cake using edible glue. Repeat for the other three drapes. For the bows, press a no. 7 ball of paste into the bow shape, remove and cut out the inside of the loops using a no. 5 piping tube. Brush these with super pearl dust and attach between the four drapes.

LACE AND DAISIES

9 Roll out some flower paste and then rub white vegetable fat (shortening) on to your board. Add the paste and press down. Rub a little fat on to the lace cutter, press into the paste and remove. Using a pin, carefully remove small sections of lace and attach around the base of both cakes using glue.

10 Cut out four small daisies from flower paste using the cutter. Place on to the soft side of a celpad and press a veining tool on to each petal. Cup the centre using the round end of a small celstick. Attach to the cake side. Pipe small dots of yellow royal icing into the daisy centres.

FINISHING TOUCHES

11 Pipe a small shell at the base of each cake and a small 'S' scroll on the top edge of the small cake. Embroider either side of the daisies using a no. 1 tube. Place a little sugarpaste into the bell and arrange mini daisies, leaves and twisted floral tape loops (see mini flower instruction on pages 140–141).

USEFUL TIPS

• This type of cake can also be made stacked with all three cakes on top of each other, to simplify the design.

• This wedding cake could be made for the bride and groom to take away on their honeymoon as a miniature version of the main wedding cake.

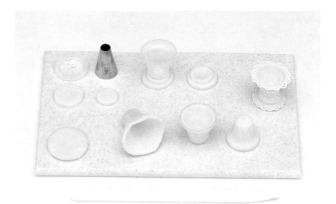

Roll out strengthened lemon paste and cut out two discs for the base of the vase. Mould a pad into a small bell mould. Dry, then decorate using royal icing.

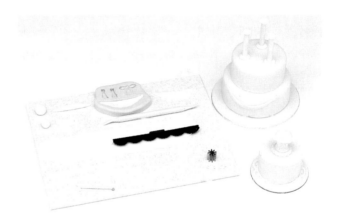

Press 50/50 paste into the drapes and bow mould. Dust with super pearl and attach to the cake. Cut out the frills and mini daisies from flower paste, then attach these to the cake.

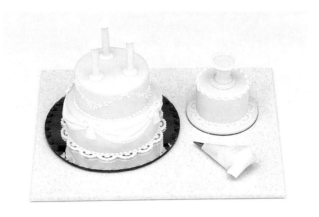

Pipe a small shell around the bases of the cakes and a small scroll design on the top tier. Pipe embroidery on each side of the small daisies with yellow royal icing piped into the centres.

Appliqué cake

The pretty appliqué design on this cake echoes the delicate shape and colours of the flowers and leaves. By placing the wire stems of the flowers inside the vase shape, the spray is easily secured to the cake and also easily removed.

COVERING THE CAKE

1 Brush the cake with apricot glaze, then cover with almond paste. Place on the cake board.

2 Cut a strip of paper 5cm (2in) wide, and long enough to stretch across the top and down both sides of the cake.

3 Brush the surface of the almond paste with clear alcohol, apart from the area where the strip of paste is to be removed.

4 Roll out the pale green sugarpaste (rolled fondant) and cover the cake and board. Leave until the surface is firm.

5 Place the strip of paper on top of the cake and, holding it in place, cut down both sides through the sugarpaste with a sharp palette knife, and remove the green paste. Brush the exposed almond paste with alcohol and insert a matching piece of white sugarpaste.

Cake and Decoration

- 23cm (9in) square cake
- apricot glaze
- 1kg (2¼lb) almond paste
- 30cm (12in) square cake board
- clear alcohol (gin or vodka)
- 1kg (2¼lb) soft mint green sugarpaste (rolled fondant)
- 150g (5oz) white sugarpaste
- 175g (6oz) flower paste (gum paste), plus small pieces of pale pink, yellow, white and green
- fern green and fuchsia pink liquid food colourings (SF)
- light green dusting powder
- aquilegia flowers (see pages 138–139)

Special Equipment

- fine palette knife
- frame mould (C)
- aquilegia leaf cutters (C)
- calyx cutters CX1 and CX2 (FFM)
- blossom cutters (5 petal) 21mm (¹³/₁₆in) and 18mm (¹¹/₁₆in)
- plain cutting wheel (PME)
- vase mould (C)
- toothbrush
- foam sponge

Hold the paper firmly in place while cutting down both sides with a palette knife before removing the strip of paste.

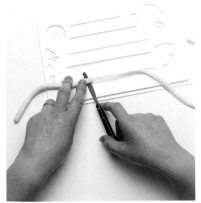

Keep pressure on the paste in the mould with your fingers as you trim away excess paste.

Cut out large leaf shapes in green paste and smaller sizes in white paste, then place one on top of the other. Vein before adding a touch of powder colour.

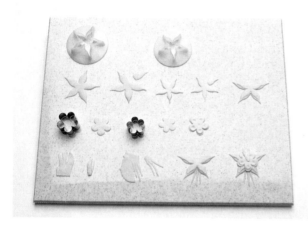

Build up the appliqué flower shapes as shown in two-tone colours using calyx and blossom cutters. Assemble the flowers using edible glue.

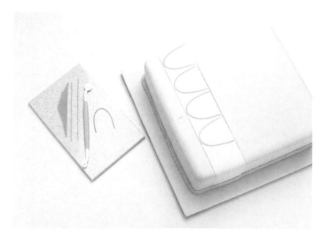

Very narrow, curved strips of green-coloured flower paste are cut out and placed along the white-coloured inlay to represent the flower stems.

DECORATING THE CAKE

6 Roll out a long thin sausage of 50/50 sugarpaste/ flower paste (gum paste) mix in a matching colour to go around the base of the cake. Dust the required strip on the frame mould with cornflour (cornstarch) and lightly press the paste into it.

7 Use the fine palette knife to trim away the excess, while holding the paste in place with your fingers. Smooth the trimmed surface to neaten.

8 Move the trimmed paste along so that another piece can be placed in the mould, matching the pattern carefully. Brush the back of the paste with water and attach around the base of the cake straight away.

LEAVES

9 Thinly roll out slightly darker green flower paste and cut out leaves with the larger aquilegia leaf cutter (approximately 12 required). Cut out the same number of small leaves in white flower paste.

10 Place a white leaf on top of each green leaf. Vein the two together with the dresden tool. Dust the leaves with light green dusting powder and attach to the cake before they are dry, so that they can be bent over the edge of the cake where necessary.

FLOWERS

11 Cut out some large calyx shapes with the calyx cutters in pale pink and smaller shapes in white, then remove one sepal from each shape. Place one on top of the other.

12 Cut out blossom shapes with the blossom cutters in yellow and white, placing the smaller white blossoms on top of the larger yellow ones.

13 Roll out pale yellow paste very thinly and cut a piece 1 x 2cm ($^3/_8$ x $^3/_4$in) long; snip one edge finely with scissors. Gather together and trim to 1.5cm ($^5/_8$in) in length to form the stamens.

14 Roll out pale pink paste very finely to 2.5 x 1.5cm (1 x $^5/_8$in) and, with scissors, cut to three fine points. These are the long spurs at the back of the flowers.

15 Assemble the flower shapes as shown, using edible glue to stick the pieces together.

16 Cut out very narrow strips of green paste 11cm (4$^{1}/_{4}$in) long using the wheel tool and, while soft, position in curves on the top and sides of the white area of the cake.

17 Attach the flowers and leaves with edible glue, bending them where necessary over the cake edges.

18 Attach flowers, leaves and stems to the two corners at the other side of the cake.

VASE

19 Dust the vase mould with cornflour, roll out 50/50 white sugarpaste/flower paste and press into the mould. Press into position using a piece of foam sponge to smooth. While holding in place, trim the paste with the fine palette knife and leave to partly dry in the mould.

20 Remove from the mould and cut away the neck section, then leave to dry completely. Brush away any cornflour remaining on the surface.

21 Mix green and pink liquid food colourings with clear alcohol, then, using a toothbrush, spatter the surface with colour.

FINISHING TOUCHES

22 Attach the vase to the cake top with softened paste and insert the assembled spray of aquilegia into the open end of the vase. See instructions for the aquilegia flowers in the flower section (pages 138–139).

USEFUL TIP

• When moulding a long strip of paste, use two polythene bags – one at each end of the mould – feeding the paste from one bag out and across the mould into the other bag after moulding. This keeps the paste soft until required.

With a small palette knife, attach a leaf shape over the join and a flower shape at the base of each curve, attaching them with softened sugarpaste.

Trim the edge of the vase neatly while making sure the paste does not slip in the mould. Take care especially with the narrow part at the neck to maintain a good shape.

After drying, the vase surface can be spattered with pink and green liquid food colouring, using a toothbrush to give a finely speckled finish.

Sugar flowers

Flowers offer a never-ending source of inspiration and form to be reproduced in sugar. Achieving the realistic detail of some flowers can be time consuming, making them expensive to produce. Other flowers can be made more simply. In this section of the book, you will find blooms that are quick-to-produce and some more challenging projects. There are a number of excellent books available that deal solely with the making of flowers, but here we show only a small selection. Like most sugarcraft projects, making flowers requires careful planning to ensure that you have the correct equipment. When a cutter is not available, however, you can sometimes use templates.

Peony

Materials

- white flower paste (gum paste) (optional)
- pink, pale moss green and moss green flower paste
- nile green floristry tape • magenta dusting powder (ISAC) • foliage green dusting powder (SF)

Special Equipment

- 20-, 24- and 26-gauge wires • size guide (C)
- 4cm (1¹/₂in) and 2.5cm (1in) styrofoam balls
- peony petal set (ISAC, C) • no. 18 veiner (ISAC, C)
- 4cm (1¹/₂in) and 2.5cm (1in) five-petal blossom cutters (ISAC, C) • peony leaf set (ISAC, C)• single peony leaf cutter (ISAC, C) • peony leaf veiner (ISAC, C)

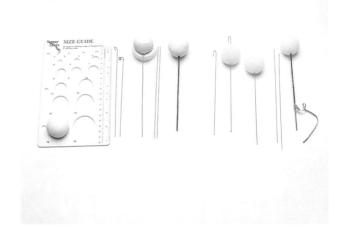

1 For a paste centre, hook a 20-gauge wire and wrap around the end of pliers, forming an 'e' shape. Brush with egg white and push into a no. 15 ball of white paste. Mould at the base and dry for 1–2 days. Once dry, add two more 20-gauge wires and tape down. For a styrofoam ball, hook the wire, dip in hot glue and insert into a ball. Add 2 x 20-gauge wires, tape down and continue immediately.

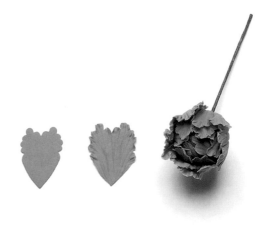

2 Cut out six small pink petals. Press on to the no. 18 veiner. On the same side as the veining, work the edge using a dresden tool, on the coated side of the celpad working from the inside outwards. Turn over the pad and work from the outside of the petal to the inside to slightly cup. Attach two petals overlapping on top of the centre ball, covering completely. Attach remaining petals.

3 Roll out some more pink flower paste and cut out five medium-sized petals from the petal cutter set. Work these in exactly the same way as the smaller petals described in caption 2. Attach these five medium petals into a spiral shape to the petals on the ball, hanging the peony upside down to dry a little before continuing. A pasta machine can be used to roll out the paste evenly.

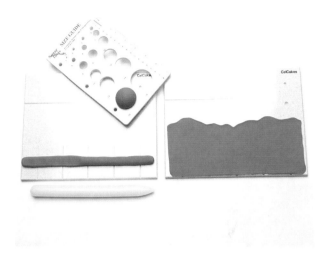

4 Continue rolling out more paste and cut out five large petals. Cut 1cm (¹/₂in) off the base of each petal. Repeat as for the previous petals, then pleat the square end of the petal. Attach these five petals again in a spiral, overlapping the previous five petals. Then continue with five more large-sized petals but do not cut from the base of these five. Attach the petals to the flower.

5 To make five large-sized peony petals, take a no. 15 ball of pink paste (measured in the size guide), roll into a sausage and place over the five ridges of the large celboard. Flatten the sausage and then dust a little cornflour (cornstarch) on top. Roll up towards the centre of the board and down towards the base. Remove the paste and turn over on to a work board.

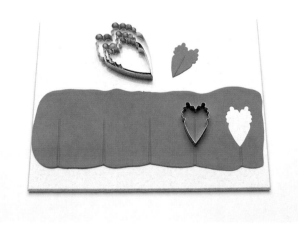

6 Cut out five large-sized petals. Take a 26-gauge white wire dipped into egg white and insert 2.5cm (1in) into the ridge. Mould at the base of the petal and place ridge-side then flat-side on to the no. 18 veiner. Work the edge on the flat side as for the previous petals. Bend the wire a little using thumb and finger, then bend the wire at right angles using pliers.

7 Loosely tape these petals around the flower centre as shown, in an upside down position, so that the petals will dry at the correct angle and shape. Continue with five extra large petals made in the same way but use 24-gauge wire for these larger petals. Leave both sets of petals to dry for 2–3 hours, then untape and place on crate foam to continue drying.

8 For a bud, prepare a 2.5cm (1in) styrofoam ball or no. 12 ball of paste as for the centre, add 2 extra wires and tape down. Cut out 6 small petals. Attach 2 petals, then 2 each side as for the first stage of the flower, overlapping more. Cut a 2.5cm (1in) 5-petal blossom in moss green. Cut in between each petal using scissors and slightly thin and soften edges. Attach to the back of the bud.

9 Tape the dry petals around the centre. These can be dusted first with magenta dusting powder, or after the calyx is put on, depending on the vibrancy of the petals. Roll out some pale moss green and make the calyx for the flower as for the bud but use a 4cm (1¹/₂in) cutter. Once the flower, bud and calyxes have dried slightly, dust a little darker green around the base of the calyx.

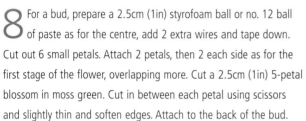

10 Roll moss green paste over the grooves of the board, cut out single and sets of leaves. When cutting out sets, flip the smaller side cutter to make a pair of leaves. Dip 24-gauge wire into egg white and insert into the large and single leaves; use 26-gauge wire on the smaller side leaves. Mould at the base of the leaf. Place the flat side on the leaf veiner, then soften the edges of the leaf on the ridge side. Hollow the leaf base on the flat side using a veining tool. To finish the leaves, dry on foil to give a natural shape. Tape the leaves together and dust using foliage green dusting powder. Steam the leaves to set the colour and brush with white vegetable fat (shortening) or glaze.

Periwinkle

Materials

- white flower paste (gum paste)
- 26- and 28-gauge white wires
- lavender, bluebell and eucalyptus dusting powders
- tiny amount of pale green flower paste
- nile green floristry tape

Special Equipment

- size guide (C) • periwinkle cutter set (C)
- no. 41 veiner (C) • fine needle tool (C)
- small lily former (C) • small and medium ball tool
- grooved board • skimmia leaf cutter set (C)

1 Roll a size 7 paste ball to a teardrop, place the point into the medium hole on a celpad, roll out thinly. Cut out petals and vein. Open up the centre, indent five times with needle tool and insert a hooked 28-gauge wire. Dry in a former. Dust with lavender and bluebell. Insert a 28-gauge wire into a size 4 paste ball for a bud. Pinch five times lengthwise with tweezers, spiral bud edges around.

2 Roll white paste over a grooved board and cut out various-sized leaves. Insert a $^1/5$ length 28-gauge wire into the wide end and vein. Place face down on a foam pad surface and soften the edges with a small ball tool. When dry, dust leaves with eucalyptus to give a variegated appearance, leaving the edges white. Cut out calyces in light green paste and attach to flowers and buds.

3 With $^1/3$ width green tape, wrap several times around the end of a 26-gauge wire and continue down the wire, adding leaves in pairs, close to the stem. Buds and flowers grow singly or in groups on short stems and should be added at intervals with the leaves. When dusting petals, placing the tip of a cotton bud in the flower throat prevents colour getting into the throat.

Peony wedding cake

With its oriental influence, this cake has been made in an unusual colour combination and is ideal for a wedding or any celebration. The design shows that one large focal flower works well in a spray with foliage and filler flowers.

1 Roll out the pale pink sugarpaste (rolled fondant) and texture with the linen roller. Cover the boards. Place the smaller board on the larger one and cover the cakes with the pink sugarpaste. Position the cakes and trim the boards with ribbon.

PEARLS AND FLOWERS

2 For the pearls, take 115g (4oz) of the pink paste and add the tylose or CMC and a little white vegetable fat (shortening). Knead, then place in a plastic bag for 2 hours. Make the pearls in the bead maker (see page 66). Position the pearls around the base of both cakes.

3 Make up the sprays and insert the top spray into the posy holder. Add organza ribbon to fill any gaps. Position on the cake.

Cake and Decoration

- 2kg (4¹/₂lb) pale pink sugarpaste (rolled fondant)
- 32cm (12in) teardrop-shaped cake
- 13cm (5in) round cake
- 42 x 37cm (16 x 14in) oval cake board
- 37 x 32 cm (14 x 12in) oval cake board
- periwinkle blue ribbon to trim cake boards
- 2.5ml (¹/₂ teaspoon) tylose or CMC
- white vegetable fat (shortening)
- peony and periwinkle (see pages 122–125)
- pink sheer organza ribbon

Special Equipment

- linen roller (HP)
- 6mm (¹/₄in) bead maker (CK)
- posy holder

■ Wire the peony bud, leaves and periwinkle sprays to the main peony flower stem and insert into the posy holder.

■ For the bottom spray, cut the wires short. Attach a ball of sugarpaste into the cake hollow with glue. Position the spray.

Montana clematis

Materials

• light green floristry tape • pale yellow, violet and moss green flower paste (gum paste) • fine white silk stamens (ISAC) • primrose, spring green, apple green, deep purple, white and burgundy dusting powders (SF)
• royal purple dusting powder (ISAC)

Special Equipment

• 20-, 22-, 24-, 26- and 28-gauge wires
• size guide (C) • clematis flower and leaf cutters (ISAC, C) • silicone dogwood press (SB, ISAC)
• celformers set 1 (ISAC, C) • clematis leaf veiner (ISAC, C)

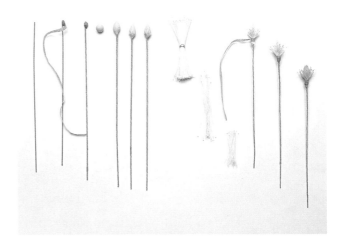

1 Tape the end of a 24-gauge wire five times with ¹/₃ width tape. Make a hook and tape over five times. Continue down the wire. Taking a no. 4 ball of yellow paste, brush egg white on the tape, insert into ball. Mould at base, make into a cone and snip. Cut a ¹/₆ bunch of stamens in half and tape around cone base. Trim and work down. Dust stamens pale primrose then spring green in centre.

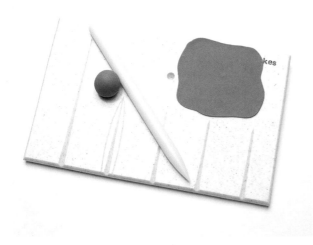

2 For each clematis flower, take a no. 10 ball of violet flower paste (gum paste), using the size guide. Roll the violet paste over the medium hole on a celboard. Once rolled over, remove the paste and turn over. This will give you a small 'hat' on the back of the piece of paste. This technique is used for flowers with shallow backs.

3 Taking the larger of the two clematis flower cutters, cut out the flower shape from the violet flower paste with the hat positioned in the centre. Make sure you position the hat in the centre of the shape to give the centre of the flower strength as the flower petals are narrow in the centre. (This technique is used for flowers such as hydrangea, dogwood etc.)

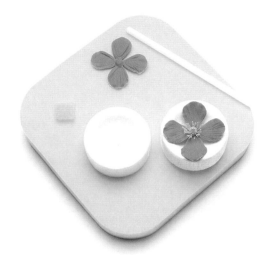

4 Place the flower shape into the silicone dogwood press as shown, pressing the two halves of the press together. Then place on the soft side of the celpad with the hat towards you. Make a loop from 20-gauge wire taped together. Hold and press this on to the back of each petal to give realistic veining. This technique can be used on other flower petals and leaves.

5 Soften petal edge on hat side using the rounded end of the large celstick. Hollow the centre on the flat side using the rounded end. Brush egg white on to the stamens base, thread the flower up the wire, and mould at the base. Slide a foam square up the wire, then a medium former. Turn over and use a paperclip to support. The foam stops flowers drying too cupped. Dry in former.

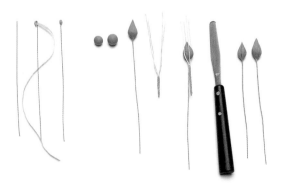

6 When making the smaller half-open clematis flowers, repeat all the instructions for producing the main flower but use the smaller-sized clematis flower cutter. Dry each finished smaller clematis flower in a small lily former to create a more closed-up flower, as shown in the photograph. For an even more closed-up flower, dry upside down.

7 For buds, tape and hook the wire as in step 1 using 28-gauge wire and 1/3 width tape. Brush the tape bud with egg white and insert into nos. 5 or 6 balls of paste. Mould at base, then mould to a cone. Make a cage with 4 x 26-gauge wires by taping at one end. Pull the cone down into the wire cage, then pull wires to divide the cone into four. Mark lines on each section, remove the cage and dry.

8 Roll pale green paste over the grooves on a celboard. Remove, turn over and cut out small and large leaves. Insert 28-gauge wire, dipped in egg white, on side leaves and 26-gauge wire into larger ones. Mould at leaf base and place each leaf, flat-side down, on the veiner, pressing with foam. Soften the leaf edge. Turn over and vein down the centre on foam. Hollow the leaf base. Dry on foil.

9 Once dry, tape the base of each clematis leaf using green floristry tape. Assemble the leaves into groups of three as shown. Dust the leaves with apple green dusting powder and a little burgundy dusting powder to highlight the leaves. Steam each leaf gently to set the colour, then brush each leaf with white vegetable fat (shortening) or glaze to finish.

10 Colour flowers and buds using royal purple dust, deep purple, then burgundy on the petal edges to highlight. Dust apple green mixed with white dust at the base of the flowers and buds. Assemble on to a 22-gauge wire and, as the groups are taped together, dust a little burgundy powder on to the tape. Once assembled, steam the flowers, buds and stems to set the colour.

USEFUL TIPS

• These clematis petal and leaf cutters can be used for several other flowers and leaves. Use the petal cutters for dogwood flowers and all-in-one poppy flowers, and the leaf cutters for peony leaves and Japanese anemones. This shows how versatile certain flower cutters can be.

• Other colours of clematis, such as pink and white, can be made using the same technique.

• There are other varieties of clematis that can be made with different cutters. Some types are made with six or eight individual petals.

• The colouring shown on the clematis can be used on the iris as well.

11 The finished clematis spray also shows the pale pink clematis flower, which is a type of Montana clematis. When making the pink clematis flower, repeat as for the violet bloom but dust the completed flowers, buds and leaves with pink and pale moss green dusting powders. This pale pink clematis is very attractive on a baby cake or a summer wedding cake where pale pink is preferred.

Foliage

Materials

Silver dollar eucalyptus: • eucalyptus colour flower paste (gum paste) (SF) • 20- and 28-gauge white wires • nile green floristry tape • eucalyptus and chocolate dusting powders (SF)

Bear grass: • mid-brown 50/50 sugarpaste (rolled fondant)/flower paste, softened with extra egg white and white vegetable fat (shortening)• 28-gauge white wire

Special Equipment

Silver dollar eucalyptus: • piping tubes (tips) • geometric cutter set (FMM) • poinsettia leaf veiner (FMM)

Bear grass: • clay gun with second smallest round disc

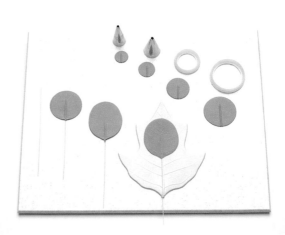

1 **Silver dollar eucalyptus:** Roll paste over celboard grooves. Turn over and cut out using piping tube ends and round cutters. Dip a 28-gauge wire into egg white and insert halfway into the ridge. Mould at base, then roll a little longer. Lay, flat-side down, on the veiner and press on to the ridge using foam. Remove and soften the edges. Hollow the leaf base using a veining tool. Dry flat.

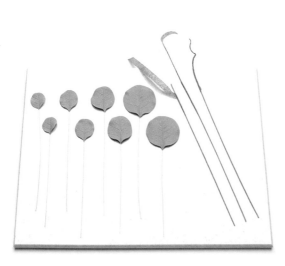

2 Once the eucalyptus leaves are dry, take ¹/₂ width green floristry tape and wrap some tape on to the end of the 20-gauge wire. Continue twisting at the end of the wire and curl this twisted floral tape using your fingers. Then, using fine tweezers, bend the stem of each pair of leaves at an angle and tape in pairs down the wire in your required formation.

3 Here the finished spray of silver dollar eucalyptus has two main stems. Once the leaves are grouped together, dust over using eucalyptus dusting powder and a dusting brush, then dust a little chocolate dusting powder on the base of the leaves and the stem. Steam over the spray of leaves to set the colour and give a natural lustre to the leaves.

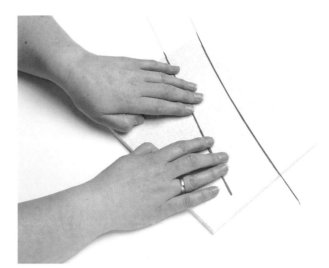

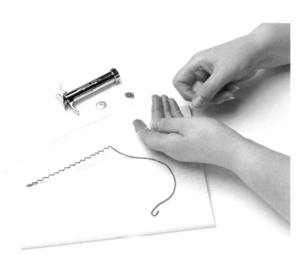

1 **Bear grass:** Before inserting the paste into the clay gun barrel, rub a little white vegetable fat (shortening) on to the surface. Extrude a length of paste and attach to the end of a full-length wire. Holding the wire in one hand, use the other hand to twist the wire so that the paste spirals around it. Take care to ensure that the spacing is even but not too wide.

2 Do not allow the paste to dry at all at this stage. Quickly place the wire on to a flat surface and, with the fingers of both hands, spread evenly apart. Roll the covered wire back and forth until the spiral of paste blends together to form a fine smooth covering. Speed is important in order to blend the paste while it is still soft so that no gaps remain.

3 While still soft, the covered lengths can be bent, curved or curled and twisted into the required shapes. Allow the pieces of bear grass to dry thoroughly before adding them to an arrangement, so that the smooth surface does not become damaged. Bear grass adds a stylish touch to all kinds of arrangements, sprays and bouquets and can be made in green paste.

USEFUL TIPS

• Extruding paste from the clay gun is made easier by softening the paste.

• When short fine leaves are required, a wire can be pushed through a disc and into the clay gun barrel, so that softened sugarpaste can be extruded along its length. A round disc or a slit disc will give different leaf shapes.

• Floral tape wrapped over wires can be used for a quick alternative to paste twigs.

• The twigs or bear grass can be made in other colours or painted silver or gold for Christmas, holidays or a wedding.

• If you do not have a clay gun, roll out paste from thin strips and wind around the wire, blending in the same way.

Gerbera daisy

Materials

- 20-gauge wires • white, pale yellow, orange and pale moss flower paste (gum paste)
- orange, red and lime dusting powders (ISAC)
- primrose yellow dusting powder (SF)

Special Equipment

- size guide (C) • gerbera daisy cutter (ISAC, C)
- daisy collection cutter set (FMM)
- silk porcelain tool (HP) • veining tool (FMM)
- celformer set A (ISAC, C)
- medium plastic stem tube (ISAC)

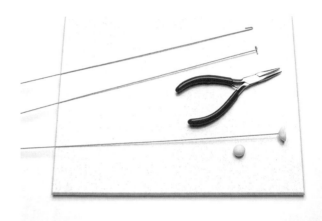

1 For the gerbera centre, make a hook about 10mm (1/3in) from the end of a 20-gauge wire. Bend halfway down the hook to create a 'T'-shape. Brush with egg white and insert into a no. 7 ball of paste. Mould at the base and flatten the top to make a no. 8 on the size guide. Leave the centre part to dry for at least 24 hours before proceeding to the next stage.

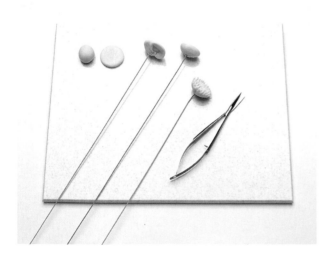

2 When dry, flatten out a no. 9 ball of pale yellow paste and brush egg white all over the dry centre. Mould the yellow part around the dry centre then, using fine scissors, snip three rings of fine cuts around the centre edge. Pinch the central area to texture using fine tweezers. Working on the soft side of a celpad, press a dresden tool on to the outside ring of snips to flatten slightly.

3 Cut out a no. 3 and 4 daisy. Lay the orange paste over the cutter and roll across. Place the daisy on to the coated celpad side and roll across using a silk porcelain tool. Place on foam and vein down the petal centres. Place the larger daisy on foam, then attach a smaller daisy, overlapping the larger petals. Cup the centre using a medium pin, then attach to the yellow centre. Dry in a former.

4 Roll out some more orange flower paste and cut out two gerbera daisy shapes. Use the silk porcelain tool and veining tool as for the smaller petals. Place one gerbera shape on to the foam. Place the second on top and, once in position, stick these together using egg white. Hollow out the centre using the rounded end of the rolling pin.

5 Place a no. 15 size foam disc into the large former, then place the petals on top. Brush egg white at the base of the first petals, then push a wire through the flower centre, pulling well down to attach to the petals. Use a paperclip to secure, then bend the wire and place into a cup to dry. Once dry, carefully remove from the former, add two 20-gauge wires and tape down.

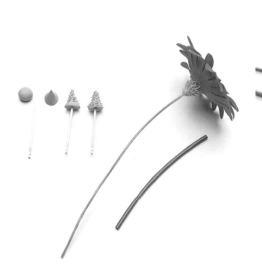

6 For the calyx, mould a no. 7 ball of green paste into a cone, like a hat, and place on to the pointed end of a cocktail stick (toothpick). Snip as shown. Push the pick through the centre. Slide up the wire and brush egg white on top. Blend on to the flower back with a veining tool. Dust with colour, then steam. If desired, use a stem tube.

7 The finished gerbera daisies are shown here. This flower is very striking and can be used in a traditional or more modern display. Because gerberas come in so many colours, they make a very versatile flower for sugarcraft. The flowers shown here are dusted using primrose and lime dusting powders in the centre, with orange, then red dust on the edges of the petals.

Crocus

Materials

- white, yellow and moss green flower paste (gum paste)
- 26- and 28-gauge white wires
- yellow, orange, lilac, violet, white and moss green dusting powders • fine white stamens
- yellow and orange textured colourings (SF)
- nile green floristry tape

Special Equipment

- size guide (C) • crocus cutters (2 sizes) (C)
- fine needle tool (C) • grooved board • medium ball tool • plain cutting wheel (PME) • no. 00 fine brush
- template (see page 190)

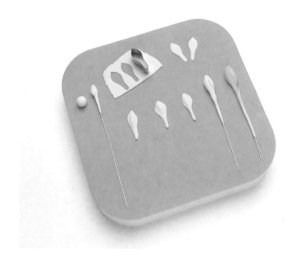

1 Place a size 6 ball of white paste on to a $^1/_3$ length hooked 26-gauge wire, tapering at the base. Roll out white paste and cut three petals with the small crocus cutter. Vein using the square end of a needle tool, working from the centre out towards the sides. Cup the petals on the reverse with the ball tool and attach while soft, tapering down the stem. Brush with yellow dusting powder.

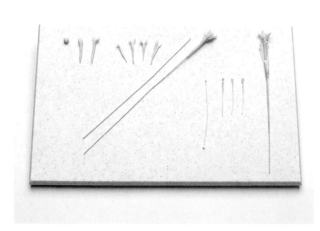

2 To make the pistil, use a size 1 ball of yellow paste, taper then flatten the wide end and snip with scissors. Frill and gather up. Make four per flower and, while soft, attach to a $^1/_3$ length wire. Allow to dry. Brush three half-length stamens with egg white and dip into textured colouring. When dry, tape around the centre, securing with a small piece of yellow flower paste.

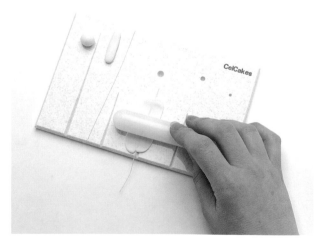

3 Take a size 7 ball of white flower paste and roll into a sausage shape, then flatten. Position along a groove in the rolling board. Place a $^1/_3$ length 28-gauge wire on top of the paste, with the wire protruding from both ends. Roll the paste lengthwise, holding the wire at both ends until it is embedded in the paste and the paste is thin enough.

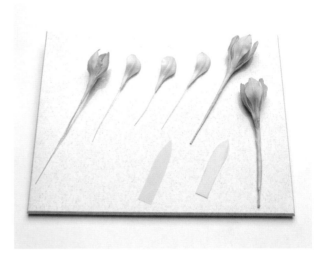

4 Remove the paste from the board, turn over and cut out a petal with the larger crocus cutter. Using the squared needle tool, vein and thin the petals. Cup on both sides of the wire to curve before cutting away the wire at the tip. Dust three petals lightly with colour while soft, then tape them around the stamen centre. Shape finely down the stem. Allow this stage to dry.

5 Make and dust three more petals, before attaching them while still soft, then taper the paste at the base. Roll out white paste finely, cut out using the sheath template and, after veining with the needle tool, attach this around the stem with egg white. Dust a very pale green, and paint fine dark green lines of varying length at the base of the petals. .

6 Roll out green flower paste over a groove in the board. Using the templates, cut out leaves of differing lengths with the cutting wheel and remove from the board. Vein down the length of the leaves with a dresden tool. Pinch down the ridge on the back, curve slightly and allow to dry. Dust the leaves with moss green dusting powder.

7 The crocus flowers can be arranged with buds and leaves in a naturally growing group in a container or placed together and laid on the top of a celebration cake (see page 17, where a paste bow is added). These flowers make the perfect decoration for a springtime celebration cake.

Aquilegia (columbine)

Materials

- white and mid-green flower paste (gum paste)
- 26- and 30-gauge white wires
- pink, moss green, lemon, lime green and foliage green dusting powders
- nile green floristry tape
- fine yellow stamens

Special Equipment

- size guide (C)
- aquilegia cutter set (C)
- fine needle tool (C)
- no. 41 veiner (C)

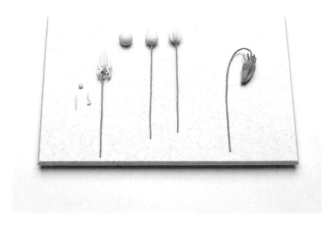

1 For buds, roll a size 1 ball of white paste to 1cm (1/2in) long, tapering at the ends. Curl one end inwards and dry. Insert a 1/3 length 26-gauge hooked wire into a size 5 ball of paste and form into a cone. Pinch with tweezers to form five ridges. Brush the spike tips with egg white and insert between the ridges. When dry, dust the buds with pink and moss green powder.

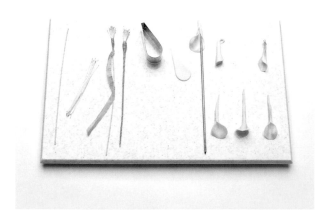

2 Tape a small bunch of yellow stamens to a 1/2 length 26-gauge wire. Cut out five petals and vein by rolling the square end of the needle tool from side to side on both surfaces. Curl the petals around the needle tool, rolling to a fine tapered point. For open flowers, curve the petal edges backwards. For closed flower, roll more tightly and curve points inwards. Dust lemon and pink.

3 Roll out white paste over a grooved board and cut out five petals. Insert a 1/4 length 30-gauge wire into each. Vein both sides of each petal with the needle tool and curl the sides inwards at the base on the ridged side. When dry, dust with pink fading to white towards the tip. Dust lime green on the tips. Tape the petals firmly around the stamen centre with 1/3 width tape.

4 Soften some flower paste (gum paste) by adding a little egg white to make a sticky glue. Apply a small amount between each of the five outer petals and attach a tubular yellow petal in each gap to complete the aquilegia flower.

5 Roll out green paste over a grooved board, cut out leaves using both cutter sizes and insert a 1/4 length 30-gauge white wire. For small, simple leaf shapes, cut down leaves as shown. Vein on the no. 41 veiner and soften the edges on the reverse side, using a foam pad surface. When dry, assemble one large and two small leaves together and dust with moss and foliage green.

6 To begin the assembly of the spray, collect the flower heads and buds together, taping with 1/3 width nile green floristry tape. Add two or three small leaves where the flower and bud stems join. Arrange the aquilegia flowers into sprays with groups of large leaves. Page 117 shows the flowers used on a cake with complementary appliqué design.

Miniature flowers

Lily: For the centre, use three fine stamens bent in half and a longer one for the pistil, taped to a 30-gauge wire. Cut out two sets of petals in orange flower paste and vein down the petal centres. Place the petals on top of each other and cup on soft sponge before inserting the stamen centre. For buds, insert a wire into a size 2 ball of paste, taper and mark three times with tweezers.

Primula: Take a size 5 ball of pink paste, press over the smallest hole in the celboard and roll thinly. Remove, turn over and cut out mini primrose petals. Cut out a mini 5-petalled blossom and press on to the flower centre. Insert a 30-gauge wire and secure. Indent each petal centre. Cut out a calyx with the mini calyx cutter. Dust flowers with plum and lime green powder centres.

Pansy and violet: Roll a size 4 ball of yellow paste over the smallest hole in the celboard to create a 'bulb' for the flower back. Cut out and stretch the petals, then insert a 30-gauge wire. Dust, then paint black markings with a fine brush. Paint on a calyx with moss green. For the violet, stretch petals lengthwise and pinch to a narrower shape. Make leaves by rolling paste over a grooved board.

Fern and ivy: Slightly flatten a small sausage of green paste and roll over, leaving a ridge on one side. Cut out using the mini fern and ivy cutters. Take a 30-gauge wire, brush a little egg white on to the end and insert into the leaf. Press a veining tool in the leaf centre to give a 'V' shape. Once dry, tape the leaves together using 1/4 width tape. Dust or paint as required.

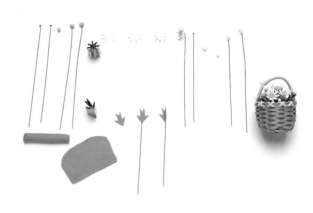

Orchid: Hook a 30-gauge wire, brush with egg white and insert into a no. 2 ball of paste. Mould into a carrot shape, flatten and pinch the top with tweezers. Dry a little, then cut out the throat and back. Frill the throat and two wider petals. Mark a vein down the throat middle and petals. Gently cup the head forward and the other petals back. Attach the throat to the back petals and slide up wire of column and attach. For buds, hook a 30-gauge wire and insert into nos. 1 – 2 balls of paste. Mould to a balloon shape, mark five times using a knife. For leaves, roll a no. 3 paste ball on to a wire, roll into a long tube, shape and flatten. Make roots from twisted white tape.

Daisy: Make a T hook on a 30-gauge wire. Brush with egg white, insert into a no. 2 ball of yellow paste. Pinch back with tweezers, brush centre top with egg white and dip into yellow pollen (semolina with yellow dust). Dry. Cut out white paste daisies. Vein and cup each petal. Slide daisy up the wire and secure. Dry, paint the calyx with green and alcohol. For buds, hook the wire, brush with egg white and insert into nos. 1 – 2 balls of paste. Pinch eight times using tweezers. Make calyx as flowers and leaves as ivy or fern.

Flowers can be arranged into a tiny container made from sugar, a basket, a plant pot or other miniature vessel. They are also very effective in small wired sprays and groups. Alternatively, flower heads and leaves without wires can be used to make tiny delicate swags and designs on cake sides.

GUEST AUTHOR

TOSHIE HARASHIMA

Royal Icing

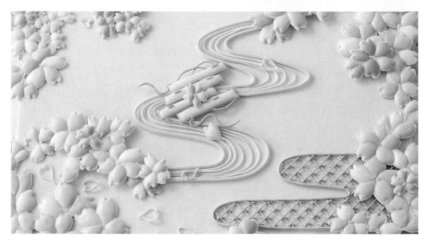

Covering and decorating cakes in royal icing gives
them a beauty which is neat and clean.
It is also a good medium for expressing traditional
Japanese designs. It is important that royal icing
has a good finish and this can only be achieved by
carefully controlling the hand pressure when
coating and piping.

ROYAL ICING DESIGNS

These four designs are suitable as side decorations for cakes, but they can also be used for the top of the cake. It is difficult to complete these designs without a template to copy. It is best to first draw a design on the surface of the cake or to pipe on wax paper with a template underneath. To make a design larger or smaller, use a photocopier.

CONSISTENCY OF ROYAL ICING

Coating consistency: It is better to use royal icing that is not freshly made. Fresh icing can be used for the first coat, but it is easier to achieve a smooth finish with 3-4 day old icing. The thickness of the icing should be like rich honey. For the cake board, it is also easier to use runout icing that has been made in advance.

Runout consistency: Add water or fresh egg white to dilute royal icing and mix gently. Scoop the icing with a spatula and drop it back into the bowl. Lines should merge and disappear on counting to 10 – this thickness is generally considered to be 'standard'. The consistency is changed for different purposes. Thicker runout, counting 15 to 20, is suitable for curved pieces.

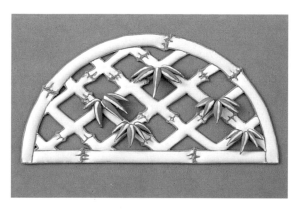

Bamboo has been regarded as a sacred tree since olden times. For this reason, a variety of bamboo designs are used for weddings (see page 144).

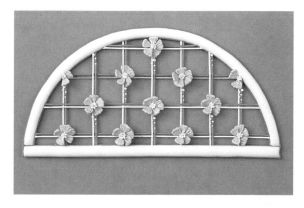

Latticework, or check-stripe, is a pattern used for doors, windows and fabrics. There are many variations; this one shows an example of double check-stripe (see page 145).

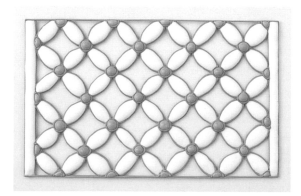

Hoshi-Shippo is a pattern created by laying quarter circles one on top of another (see page 146). These circles indicate peace and harmony. The small circles represent stars.

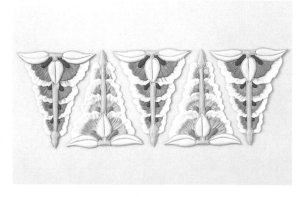

Wisteria is Japanese in origin and has been acclaimed for its strong force of life. This flower design is used in sugarcraft in many ways (see page 147).

BAMBOO DESIGN

As the bamboo grows straight up to the sky, it is regarded as a sacred plant in Japan. Bamboo lattice is used for fences, dividers or screens in the garden. As well as its practical uses, it also makes attractive decorations to enhance the beauty of many plants.

This design can be used as a cake side decoration or to cover the entire cake. You can use the same colour of royal icing for the outline and flooding.

It looks more natural to select a lighter green or moss green as well as cream.

To emphasise the bamboo joints, fill with a little less amount of runout icing and use standard runout icing for the lattice.

For the bamboo leaves, use thicker icing (count to 15 rather than 10) as it is does not have an outline. The consistency for the leaf and the vein needs to be same. They look as one body and the vein is a part of the leaf.

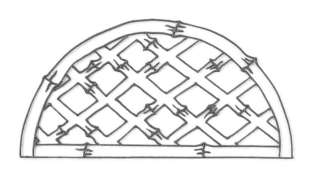

Pipe the outlines. Pipe the frame first, then inside lattice design. Pipe the short joining lines clearly to bring out the nodes of the bamboo.

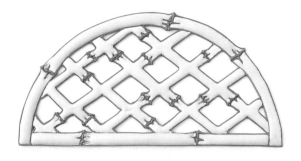

Fill the inside of the design with runout icing. Once the surface has dried, run in the frame. Do not overfill because it is more attractive when the outline is visible.

For the bamboo leaves, pipe leaf shapes with green runout icing. Pipe a line with ivory runout icing for the vein, while the green icing is still wet. Allow to dry.

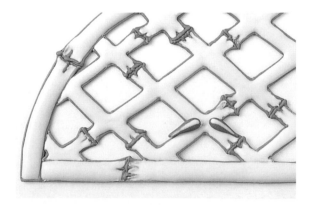

Use just a little royal icing to attach the piped bamboo leaves to the lattice runout to create a three-dimensional bamboo design.

LATTICE DESIGN

The lattice pattern has been used for textiles since ancient times. There are many varieties which combine different colours and thicknesses.

Either pipe on to wax paper and then transfer, or pipe directly on to the cake surface. Use a template underneath the wax paper for the transfer method; mark dots on the cake surface if you are using the direct method.

It is important to pipe the lines straight to make the lattice look neat. This design can be used on part of the cake or over the whole surface. The brush embroidered flower is just an accessory and could be changed to another motif to match the theme of the cake. The frame is necessary, especially when using the transfer method, to keep the latticework fixed; a runout frame is effective as it is strong. The consistency of the runout icing is standard (to a count of 10). A runout frame gives depth to the lattice design.

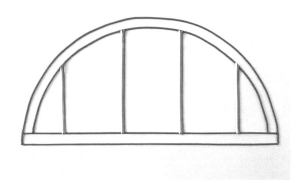

■ Pipe the frame, then pipe the vertical lines. Pipe a white line, then a pink line very close to the white. Pipe the next pair alternately.

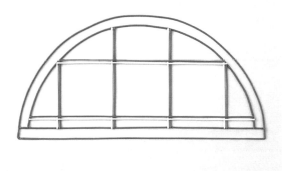

■ To continue, pipe the horizontal lines within the frame. Pipe a line in white and then in pink alternately, as for the vertical lines.

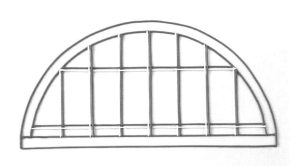

■ Pipe the vertical lines in between and then the horizontal lines. This lattice is then decorated with three-dimensional blossom flowers.

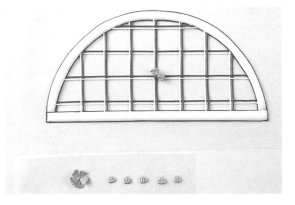

■ Pipe the petal outlines on wax paper, then brush the piped icing to achieve a petal shape. When dried, peel off. To assemble the flowers, pipe a dot and then insert the petals into it.

HOSHI-SHIPPO DESIGN

The *shippo* pattern is constructed from small circles of the same size, positioned at a quarter of the circumference of a larger circle. The circle named *shippo* represents harmony and the small circles at the crossing of the *shippo* circles represent *hoshi* meaning 'star' in Japanese.

Fill the spaces with standard runout icing (consistency count 10). The circles, because they are very small, need to be filled well since it is easy for the runout icing to dry with a hole in it. This happens when air is trapped in between the wax paper and runout icing as it is piped. One way to avoid this is to pipe normal royal icing in the bottom half of the space, and then to fill the top half with runout icing.

To have a nice shiny risen surface on a runout makes an attractive finish.

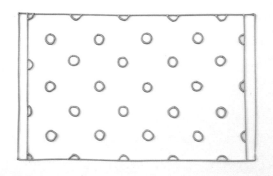

For the hoshi-shippo pattern, first pipe the frame. Next, pipe the circles, evenly spaced apart. Try to produce neatly piped circles to create an even design.

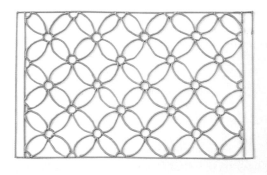

Pipe the curved lines, making sure that all the lines are connected. Pipe another layer of circles, just on top of the first layer. This raises up the circles, giving a three-dimensional effect.

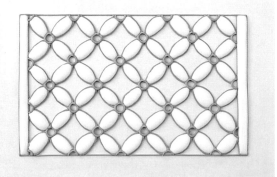

Fill the oval shapes with runout icing. Slightly overfill the shapes with runout icing so they stand up above the outline to give an attractive finish.

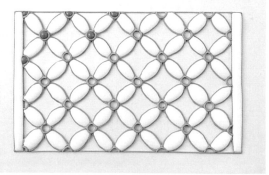

Fully fill each circle with runout icing. Add sufficient icing to keep the centres standing proud. Colour the centres, if preferred.

WISTERIA DESIGN

Wisteria has become a popular pattern in Japan. This is partly due to the fact that the name refers to a person well versed in the ancient court and military traditions of some 1000 years ago. This pattern makes an extremely attractive border decoration.

Pipe the design on to wax paper using a template underneath. Once dried, peel off and stick the design on to the cake surface. This is the easiest way to position the pieces. To avoid breakages, make sure that all the parts are joined. Use standard royal icing for the brush embroidery. For the leaf and stem, use runout icing (consistency count 10). Pipe several generous dots of icing at the back of the leaves and stem to stick them on to the cake surface. Press gently, but position firmly.

◼ For petals, pipe the outline of the outer petal in pale-coloured royal icing using a no. 2 piping tube (tip). Brush royal icing with a flat paintbrush for a petal vein.

◼ Pipe an outline for the inner petal in darker royal icing using a no. 2 tube. Brush the royal icing. Pipe a shell shape in dark icing using a no. 2 tube for the centre.

◼ After six sets of petals have been made in varying sizes, pipe the outline of the leaves and stem in green royal icing using a no. 1 piping tube.

◼ Finally, fill in the leaf design with pale green runout icing and leave to dry (see also page 143). Use darker green runout icing for stem.

Cherry blossom celebration cake

The cherry season is one of the most beautiful times of the year and a very precious time for the Japanese. This fresh-looking royal iced cake is suitable for any celebration in the springtime.

COATING THE CAKE

1 Brush the top of the cake with apricot glaze, then cover the cake top with almond paste.

2 Brush the two opposite sides of the cake with apricot glaze and cover with almond paste. Cover the other two sides of the cake with almond paste. Place the cake on the cake board and leave overnight to dry.

3 Coat the cake top with pale green royal icing. Allow to dry. Coat the two opposite sides of the cake with royal icing. Once they are dry, coat the remaining sides. Leave to dry.

Cake and Decoration

- 18cm (7in) square cake
- apricot glaze
- 800g (1¼lb) almond paste
- 30cm (12in) square cake board
- 1kg (2¼lb) pale green royal icing
- white royal icing coloured with green, pink and blue food colourings
- 1.5m 1.5cm (⅝in) wide green ribbon to trim cake board

Special Equipment

- templates (see page 196)
- nos. 0, 1 and 2 piping tubes (tips)
- greaseproof paper piping bags
- wax paper
- flower petal former

■ Pipe the outline of the flower on wax paper. Run in alternate petals. Allow to dry. Fill the remaining petals and leave to dry.

■ Pipe the raft outline on wax paper. Run the icing into alternate bars. Dry, then fill the remaining bars. Pipe short lines on the bars.

■ For the stream, pipe the outside line first, then pipe the inside lines to make a curve. Make sure all the lines are connected.

■ Pipe the cloud outline. Pipe the lines in one direction, then pipe lines on top in the other direction. Pipe short lines at each crossing.

4 Cover the cake with a second coat of pale green royal icing in the same way. Lastly, coat the cake board in pale green royal icing and allow to dry.

CHERRY BLOSSOM RUNOUTS

5 To make cherry blossom runout pieces, first make up two shades of pink standard runout icing. Place wax paper on a wooden or work board. Pipe the outline of the flower using a piping bag fitted with the no. 1 piping tube (tip) and pink royal icing. Fill in alternate petals with runout icing. Leave the surface to dry. Fill in the remaining alternate petals with the other shade of pink and leave to dry. Fill the last petal.

RAFT

6 To make the raft, lay a small piece of wax paper on a wooden or work board. Pipe the outline of the raft and strings using a piping bag fitted with the no. 1 piping tube and green royal icing. Fill alternate bars in paler green runout icing. Allow to dry. Run in the rest of the bars. Pipe the short lines on top of the bars using the no. 1 piping tube. Leave them to dry.

STREAM

7 For the stream, use two piping bags fitted with no. 1 and no. 2 piping tubes and blue royal icing. Lay wax paper on a wooden or work board. Pipe the outer lines first using the no. 2 piping tube, then pipe the inner lines to make a nice curve with the no. 1 piping tube. Make sure all the lines are connected. Leave the piped stream to dry.

CLOUDS

8 Pipe the decorative cloud design on wax paper laid on a wooden or work board. Pipe the frame with a piping bag fitted with a no. 1 piping tube and green royal icing. Pipe the lattice by piping the lines in one direction, then pipe on top in the other direction. Pipe short lines at every crossing. Overpipe the frame. Leave to dry.

FINISHING TOUCHES

9 To make heart-shaped curved petals, use a flower petal former. As soon as the petals are piped on to wax paper, place the paper in a former and stick down to secure. Pipe some petals with the outline only and fill others with icing. Leave to dry.

10 Once all the cherry blossom, stream, clouds, petals and raft pieces are dried, peel off the wax paper ready for decorating the cake.

11 First, using a palette knife to lift, carefully position the clouds using small dots of pale green royal icing.

12 Next, stick the stream into position with a small amount of green royal icing. Position the raft in the centre of the cake.

13 Lastly, arrange the blossoms and petals on the cake, using various amounts of royal icing to give them slightly different heights on the cake for a three-dimensional effect.

14 Trim the cake board with the green ribbon, securing with a non-toxic glue stick.

PROFESSIONAL TIPS

• Pipe only a small amount of royal icing at the centre of the wider petals to avoid the runout icing sinking down.

• Do not overfill the petals with runout icing or the outline of the flower will be spoiled.

• Do not press pieces too hard when securing them to the cake as they are easily broken.

• Use very small amounts of royal icing for sticking pieces down.

■ For the curved petals, use a flower petal former. As soon as the petals are piped, place in the former and stick down to secure.

■ To decorate the cake, secure the decorative pieces on the cake surface with royal icing. Use a palette knife to lift the pieces.

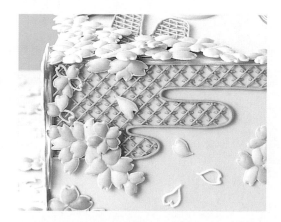

■ To create a three-dimensional effect, pipe generous amounts of icing on the backs of some of the pieces to give different heights.

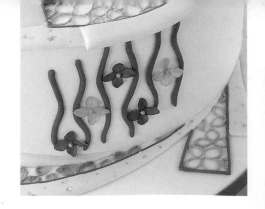

Hydrangea wedding cake

This stunning cake features the hydrangea, an original Japanese flower, and traditional celebration symbols. The collar pattern is called noshime – *a symbol for long life. The wavy lines on the sides are called* tatewaku *and indicate rising fortunes.*

COATING THE CAKES

1 Brush the tops of the cakes with apricot glaze, then cover the cake tops with almond paste.

2 Brush the cake sides with apricot glaze and cover with a strip of almond paste. Place the cakes on the cake boards and leave overnight to dry.

3 Coat the cakes with cream royal icing. Dry overnight.

4 Coat the cakes a second time with cream royal icing. Leave to dry for 24 hours. Coat the cake one more time and leave to dry overnight.

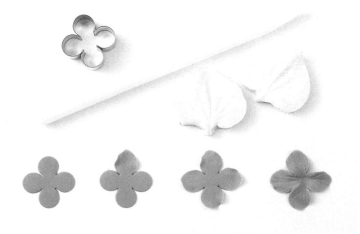

Roll out blue flower paste (gum paste) and cut out using the four-petal cutter. Work each petal with a rolling pin, then vein.

Cake and Decoration

- 18 and 27cm (7 and 11in) round cakes
- apricot glaze
- 1.8kg (4lb) almond paste
- 30 and 37cm (12 and 15in) round cake boards
- 2kg (4$^{1}/_{4}$lb) cream royal icing
- cream, green, and pale blue/lilac food colourings
- gold leaf
- 22-, 26- and 30-gauge white wires
- $^{1}/_{4}$ width floristry tape
- 115g (4oz) flower paste (gum paste)
- egg white
- blue, lilac, green and gold dusting powders
- 25g (1oz) green flower paste
- 2m 1.5cm wide blue ribbon to trim cake boards

Special Equipment

- templates (see page 195)
- nos. 0,1 and 2 piping tubes (tips)
- fine paintbrush
- 4-petal blossom cutter
- celpin
- dresden tool
- hydrangea petal and leaf veiners
- daphne cutter

152

Tape twice around the end of a 30-gauge wire, hook and tape round 3 times more. Insert into a ball of white paste. Mark lines on the top. Push through flower centre.

Roll out green flower paste and cut out the leaf shape. Insert a 26-gauge wire and vein. Make serrations on the edges with a dresden tool. Dry and dust.

Tape three flowers together, adding a 28-gauge wire. Make a bunch of nine flowers, taping into three groups. Tape the bunches together.

5 Coat the cake boards with the same cream colour royal icing. Leave to dry.

COLLARS

6 To make the collars for the cake tops, place the templates and wax paper on wooden or work boards. Pipe the outlines using a piping bag fitted with a no. 1 piping tube (tip) and cream royal icing, and another piping bag fitted with a no. 2 piping tube and green royal icing.

7 Pipe inside the design using a no. 1 piping tube and pale blue/lilac royal icing. Brush the icing with a damp paintbrush for the brush embroidery design. Fill with cream standard runout icing. Position a little gold leaf on the icing, then leave to dry for 24 hours.

8 For the cake boards, pipe the outline of the design. Pipe inside the designs, including the brush-embroidered petals. Run in directly on to the boards.

9 Pipe the wavy outline on wax paper using a piping bag fitted with a no. 1 piping tube and green royal icing for the side decoration. Fill with green runout icing, then leave to dry.

HYDRANGEAS

10 To make hydrangeas, first take a 30-gauge white wire and bind 1/4 width white floristry tape twice around the end. Bend a hook and then bind around three more times, to form a bud shape. Mould a size 1 or 2 ball of flower paste (gum paste), brush egg white on the tape bud and insert into the paste. Shape the base, mark four times with a craft knife and leave to dry. You will need 45 for each flower.

11 Roll out thin blue flower paste (but not too thinly). Cut out the petals with the four-petal blossom cutter. Work the petals with a celpin on the coated side of a celpad, to make them longer and wider. Soften the edge on the soft side of the pad. Vein using the veiner.

12 Brush egg white at the base of a tape bud. Insert the wire at the centre of the petals. Secure, then hang to dry. Colour the petals with dusting powder.

13 For leaves, roll the green flower paste over the ridges on a celboard. Cut the shape, insert a 26-gauge wire, then secure and vein. Make the serrated edges using the dresden tool on the soft side of the celpad. Soften the edges, dry and then dust green. Brush with a tiny amount of softened white vegetable fat (shortening).

14 Tape three flowers together with green floristry tape, adding a 28-gauge wire. Make a group with three bunches, adding a 22-gauge green wire to strengthen. Tape five groups of flowers together. Add the leaves.

BLOSSOMS

15 Thinly roll out blue flower paste. Cut out blossoms using the daphne cutter. Work each petal with a celpin on the soft side of the celpad. Leave to dry, then dust.

FINISHING TOUCHES

16 Peel the collars from the wax paper. Pipe with cream royal icing on the cake top edge. Position the collars.

17 Remove the green wavy pieces from the wax paper. Pipe a small amount of cream royal icing at the back, then stick to the side of the cake. Position the blossoms in between lines with cream royal icing. Pipe a small dot at the centre of the flower. Set the hydrangeas on the cakes. Trim the boards with ribbon.

PROFESSIONAL TIPS

- All the piped lines and brush-embroidered petals must be joined.
- Steam dusted flowers to set the dusting powder.
- Dust piped petals for collar work before peeling from wax paper.
- Use softened paste to set flower stems on the cake.

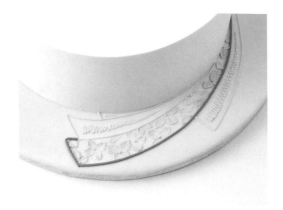

Pipe the outline of the pattern. Pipe inside the design in a zig-zag line. Pipe, then brush-embroider the petals using a fine paintbrush.

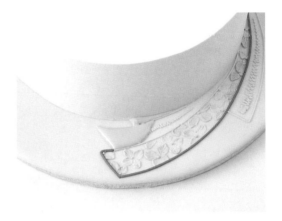

Finally, fill the design with cream runout icing and leave to dry thoroughly. Enough runout icing is needed to reach to the bottom of the cake.

Pipe the wavy outline on wax paper and then fill with runout icing. Dry. For the petals, cut out using the daphne cutter. Work the petals, dry, dust and stick.

GUEST AUTHORS

EARLENE MOORE
STEVEN STELLINGWERF

American Cakes

American cakes are made in all kinds of flavours. The most popular decorating medium is still buttercream, but the elegance of sugarpaste (rolled fondant) is changing the opinion of American cake decorators as it allows more creativity and originality in cake design. Chocolate ganache and rolled buttercream are also favourite choices.

ROLLED BUTTERCREAM ICING TECHNIQUE

Rolled buttercream has become a very popular medium for icing celebration cakes in the last 10 years. This is because the recipe is very simple to make and rolled buttercream is a very forgiving icing to work with.

First, position the cake on the cake board and cover completely with a thin layer of regular buttercream icing. The rolled buttercream will adhere to the cake with this coating.

Roll out one recipe of rolled buttercream (see page 187). Lay a thick sheet of plastic (upholstery plastic is good) on to the work surface. Form the rolled buttercream into a thick disc and lay it in the centre of the plastic. Lay a second sheet of plastic on top. With a rolling pin, start in the centre of the icing disc and roll outwards to form a circular shape. Roll out evenly to a thickness of 6–10mm ($^{1}/_4$–$^{1}/_2$in).

When rolled out, flip the icing and plastic over and remove what was the bottom sheet of plastic. Lift the icing up with the top sheet and drape the icing over the cake. Gently peel back the plastic, letting the icing fall naturally down on to the top and sides of the cake.

■ When base-coating the cake, fill in any spaces where the layers meet, so that when the rolled buttercream is applied the join will not show.

■ A marble rolling pin makes rolling out much easier as less pressure will be needed. The icing is rolled out fairly thickly so the cake does not show through the icing.

■ The plastic sheets are turned over so that there are less air pockets on the cake top. Working with your hands, fold any pleats outwards and then gently downwards to work them out.

■ Before the base-coat icing is applied to the cake, you may choose to bevel the cake edges to give a more rounded effect to the top edge of the cake.

Buttercream stencils: Stencils must be designed that begin with the back colours and work towards the front colours. Using the stencil patterns on page 196, trace them individually on to sheets of mylar, wax paper or Dura-lar sheets with a permanent ink marker, leaving a minimum of 5cm (2in) on the outside of each design section.

Begin with pattern 1 and softened white buttercream icing, spread the buttercream from the outside to the inside of stencil 1. After all the edges are sealed, spread the icing evenly over the stencil cut-out. Level and smooth this area, leaving a thin coat of icing. Lift the stencil away. Air dry and then repeat with colours and patterns.

Trace the final detail lines on a piece of wax paper that will cover the entire pattern and top of the cake. Lay the wax paper on top of a piece of porous styrofoam. Using a florist pin, puncture the lines until all the details are recorded. Place the pinpricked paper carefully over the design. Using a cottonwool ball and cocoa powder, rub gently over all the pinpricked lines. Gently remove the wax paper and pipe the details with a no. 1 or 2 piping tube (tip) and black icing.

Outline all colours and add the freehand details, such as the stems and leaves of the daisies.

■ This puppy requires six stencils. Cut out each stencil with a sharp craft knife. Place stencil pattern on the top of a cake or plaque and coat with buttercream using an angled spatula.

■ Build up the picture using golden yellow for pattern 2, red for pattern 3, brown for pattern 4, black for pattern 5 and green for pattern 6.

■ After each stencil and colour has been added, carefully lift off the stencil, leaving the cut-out pattern in icing. If rough edges appear, dry the icing, then gently press down.

■ The daisies are outlined and the greenery piped for a simple finish. The puppy on the top of the cake on page 167 was finished with flower paste stems, leaves and daisies.

Making accent decorations: *Pearls* – Roll white sugarpaste (rolled fondant) to the thickness of wooden skewers or the thickest setting on a pasta machine. Cut circles with nos. 8 and 10 piping tubes (tips) for 4mm (1/6in) and 5mm (1/5in) pearls. Roll into small balls and dry on thin sponge. Shake in a small container with pearl dusting powder.

Nails – Roll chocolate sugarpaste to 1mm (1/25in) thick and press grooves about 6mm (1/4in) apart with a large spatula. Cut circles for nail heads with a no. 10 tube, centring each of the cuts over the grooved line. Dry. Paint the tops with copper dusting powder and lemon extract.

Ribbon – Roll out lime green sugarpaste and cut strips with the strip cutter. See page 166.

Rope – Soften 450g (1lb) sugarpaste with piping gel and divide into thirds, colouring 1/3 yellow, 1/3 lime green and leave 1/3 white. Roll each colour into a long roll, then place together to fit into the cookie press or clay gun. Each colour is shown in one section of the disk. See page 166.

For quick flowers – Using a Daisy Duo mould no. 7974 (SB), firmly press flower paste (gum paste) into each mould and trim off excess. Place in the freezer for 20 minutes until firm. Twist the mould to remove the daisies, then dry on wax paper.

■ Store different pearl sizes in separate containers. (See also page 166.) Nails are used on the cake on page 169. Apply the nails to the cake using tweezers and a dot of buttercream.

■ The ribbon, rope and quick daisies are shown on page 166. Paint the daisy centres with thinned piping gel and sprinkle with yellow sugar, cornmeal and gelatin mixture for pollen.

■ The pearls and quick daisies can be made in advance and stored, speeding up the cake decoration. The three-colour rope gives an interesting accent twist.

■ The diamond and line mats quickly create interesting side designs, allowing time for making accent pieces such as the nail heads shown.

Fishing creel basket cake

This amazing cake, so full of little details, makes a wonderful surprise for a fishing enthusiast. These detail items and the lid must be made and decorated in advance of baking the cakes.

CREEL LID

1 To make the creel lid, use the 23 x 38cm (9 x 15in) cardboard covered with wax paper (with the front marked where the cake corners will be rounded). Colour strong royal icing light brown using yellow, brown and avocado colourings. Using a no. 6 piping tube (tip) and brown icing, pipe two vertical lines before overpiping with a single horizontal line as shown to form the basket-weave pattern. Allow the lid to dry totally. Trim the lid with chocolate sugarpaste (rolled fondant), cut into strips, as accents. Prop the front edge of the lid 5cm (2in) higher than the back and hang the sugarpaste fastener from the front edge.

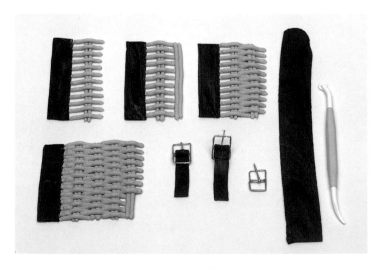

Practise piping the basket-weave design first if necessary. The straps are made from sugarpaste and the silver buckle from rice paper.

Cake and Decoration

- 23 x 38cm (9 x 15in) cardboard
- 3 egg white royal icing recipe for lid
- egg yellow, chocolate brown, avocado and black food colourings
- 1kg (2lb) brown or chocolate sugarpaste (rolled fondant) • 50g (2oz) red flower paste (gum paste) • 1kg (2lb) white flower paste • pink, green, copper, black, brown, blue, purple and avocado airbrush colours
- several large sheets rice (wafer) paper
- piping gel • miniature marshmallows
- 38 x 43cm (15 x 19in), 1cm ($1/2$in) plywood cake board • green florist foil
- five 28 x 38cm (11 x 15in) cakes
- 3kg (6lb) cream cheese buttercream icing (see page 187) • 27 x 37cm ($10^1/2$ x $14^1/2$in) and two 25 x 35cm (10 x 14in) heavy cardboard rectangles
- 4 x 15cm (6in) stress-free rings with 9cm ($3^1/2$in) long legs (SFSS)
- 50g (2oz) red and 25g (1oz) orange gumdrops • flower paste corn
- silver and gold dusting powders

Special Equipment

- nos. 804 (Ateco) and 2, 6, 7 and 10 piping tubes (tips) • airbrush
- rectangular styrofoam • 11cm ($4^3/8$in), 9.5cm ($3^3/4$in), 4cm ($1^1/2$in) circle cutters
- PVC tubing • smocking or grooved pin
- 5 x 10cm (2 x 4in) 5 bead stacker

Made from red flower paste, these pliers are easy to make if you work in stages. They are moulded and painted for a realistic look.

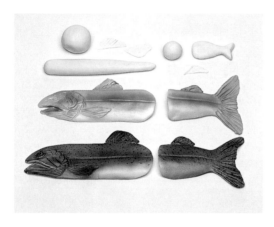

Airbrush or paint the fish in any colours you like. They are dried over rolled-up paper towels to give them a rounded shape.

This fun assortment of fishing lures are made from rice (wafer) paper and flower paste, and can be decorated in all different colours.

NEEDLE-NOSE PLIERS AND FISH

2 Form 25g (1oz) red flower paste (gum paste) into a long sausage, with one end tapered. Flatten, then cut through to make handles using a knife. Detail with a celstick and dresden tool. Paint the black section with a mix of vodka and black colouring. Brush smudges on the handle with the food colouring and a cotton swab.

3 Hand-mould the head, tail and fin sections with sugarpaste as shown using the dresden/veining tool for the detail work. Use rolled-up paper towels under the body to give the rounded shape. Airbrush the pink, green, copper and brown colourings. Use black airbrush colouring for the dots and details, painted on with a fine brush. Alternatively, paint, then dust on the colours.

4 Airbrush rectangular strips of rice (wafer) paper with colours appropriate for the lures. Cut into slim triangular strips for the lure feathers. Mould the body from a pea-sized portion of flower paste, inserting the rice-paper fish hook and ring as shown. Apply piping gel diluted with water to attach layers of rice-paper triangles representing feathers. Allow to dry between layers. Paint detail markings and eyes with food colourings and dusting powders mixed with lemon extract.

LURES, FISHING HOOKS AND BUCKLES

5 Cut a 1cm ($^{1}/_{2}$in) strip of rice paper and slip it through vodka in a dish. Lay the wet strip on wax paper and blot with a paper towel. Roll tightly from one edge and stretch it lengthwise on another sheet of wax paper on top of polystyrene (styrofoam). Pin each end with a florist pin until the length desired. For the buckles, fishing hooks and rings, form while still damp using pins into the foam to stabilise and shape.

6 Make a round bobber from a 2cm ($^{3}/_{4}$in) ball of sugarpaste wrapped around miniature marshmallows. Place on a cocktail stick (toothpick) to dry. Add a tiny strip around the middle, a flat circle on one end and a rice-paper ring on the other. The rainbow bobber is hand-moulded by pinching on the top side and opening up a mouth area. Cut the red/white spoons from paste, enclosing an elongated rice paper ring on the squared end. Cut a hole in the other end with a no. 7 tube. Dry on a spoon. Paint or airbrush.

FISHING REEL AND SALMON EGGS

7 Using cutters, the flower paste reel outer ring is cut to 11cm (4³/₈in) with a centre circle cut 4cm (1¹/₂in) in diameter; the 2nd layer narrow ring inner diameter is 9.5cm (3³/₄in). The interior holes are cut with nos. 6, 10 (Wilton) and 804 (Ateco) tubes. Cut a strip 3 x 10cm (1¹/₄ x 5in) in length for the centre section, cut oval holes with the no. 10 tube. Wrap around a wax paper covered section of PVC pipe.

8 Mould a small handle for the reel from flower paste with a piece of spaghetti inserted inside. Mark the screw in the end with the no. 10 tube and indent a line across the circle with a knife. Glue the handle on one side of the reel disc with water while wet. The spaghetti should go through all the layers. Dry, then assemble with icing. Roll a 4cm (1¹/₂in) wide long strip of flower paste with the smocking roller and wrap inside the reel for a fishing line. Paint with dusting powder mixed with lemon extract.

9 Wash the sugar from the gumdrops for the fish eggs. Place in a microwave-safe container. Heat for about 30 seconds until bubbly. Stir until one colour. Remove and place on a wax paper-covered board to cool. Place white vegetable fat (shortening) on your fingers and, when cool, pinch off small quantities and roll into balls. Leave to dry.

CREEL ASSEMBLY

10 Cover the cake board with green foil. Cut a 27 x 37cm (10¹/₂ x 14¹/₂in) piece of cardboard, rounding the front two corners. Cover with contact paper on one side. Attach to the covered board with royal icing/piping gel mixture.

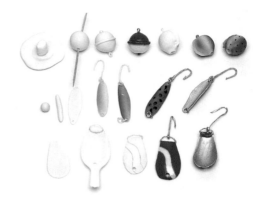

Make as many colourful bobbers, spoons and jigs as you like. The bobbers are made from sugarpaste wrapped around mini marshmallows.

For a finishing touch, before painting, add single strands made with a clay gun to make the fishing line look realistic.

The assorted edible fishing flies, jigs and bobbers make outstanding additions to the fishing basket. To give lures a shine, airbrush with diluted gum arabic solution.

The addition of bought 'worm' gums adds to the fun of the cake, giving time for making and modelling the other items.

Although the lures are fiddly to make, the recipient of the cake will be thrilled with the assortment of sugar fishing equipment you have hand-crafted.

All the fishing accessories are made in advance of baking the cake. For an alternative design, make a closed-lid creel and surround the board with a few items.

Assemble two of the cake layers on the base boards with buttercream filling. Ice the top with buttercream. Insert two of the support rings with legs side by side. Repeat with the 25 x 35cm (10 x 14in) board covered with contact paper on both sides and two more layers. Insert two more support rings. Repeat with another covered board. Cut the remaining layer at an angle leaving 5cm (2in) of flat surface on the larger section. Stack those two pieces with the smaller piece on the bottom at the back and the larger piece on top. Round the front corners on all layers of the cake, leaving the back corners squared.

11 Coat the entire cake with buttercream. Leave overnight. Ice the cake on all sides, and the back 5cm (2in) flat section with buttercream icing the same colour as the royal icing lid. Ice the angled top area with chocolate brown icing. Apply sugarpaste trim strips and buckle trims to the cake, gluing in place with water. Pipe the same basket-weave pattern on the sides of the cake and the 5cm (2in) strips across the top back of the cake. Using a toothbrush and green/brown airbrush colour, splatter dots on the sides and lid. Airbrush with the same colour to mask any icing colour differences.

12 Place the flower paste corn and gumdrop salmon eggs into the stacker bead container. Use two sections for one support and the other three sections for the other support under the lid. Pipe a line of chocolate buttercream icing at the lid and creel join. Place the lid on the top, resting the back edge in the fresh icing. Make two hinges from flower paste. Mark the centre line for the hinge and, using a no. 10 tube, mark the screw placement. Mark the line across the screws. Glue between the top back and the lid for realistic placement.

13 Make a small rope and mark to resemble the hinge joint and glue to the top of the hinge. Paint gold or silver with dusting powder and lemon extract mixture. Add large pieces first, such as the fish and the reels. When dry, decorate the cake with the remaining items.

Cake and Decoration

- 8 flower paste (gum paste) daisies, or use bought ones
- 14 quick-moulded daisies (see page 159)
- 2 x 30cm (12in) layer cake
- 29cm (11½in) cake card or cardboard covered with contact paper
- 35cm (14in) cake board or florist's foil covered board
- 1.75kg (4lb) buttercream icing (see page 186)
- 2 x 20cm (8in) layer cake
- 18cm (6in) stress-free ring support
- 19cm (7½in) cake card or cardboard covered both sides in contact paper
- puppy design (see page 158)
- brown, red, black yellow and green food colourings
- 115g (4oz) lime sugarpaste (rolled fondant)
- 450g (1lb) sugarpaste
- piping gel
- 4mm and 5mm (1/6in and 1/5in) pearls (see page 159)

Special Equipment

- cake leveler (optional)
- sugarpaste smoother
- 2cm (3/4in) dot mat (EM)
- puppy stencil (see page 196)
- strip cutter • paintbrush
- cookie press (W) or clay gun

Puppy love

Alter the stencil to suit the occasion on this beautiful springtime wedding or celebration cake, decorated with buttercream icing. Stencils give a smooth professional look to a creative design.

DECORATING THE CAKE

1 First make flower paste (gum paste) daisies, leaves and moulded daisies. Allow to dry.

2 Level the 30cm (12in) cake layers if necessary and stack on the 29cm (11½in) card or board, then position on the 35cm (14in) board. Coat with the buttercream icing.

3 Cut one 20cm (8in) layer at an angle and arrange with the high sides to the back of the cake (see www.earlenescakes.com). Assemble with the second 20cm (8in) layer and buttercream icing, using the stress-free ring support under the cake and the

█ Two kinds of daisies adorn this pretty cake. The little ones surrounding the cake top are made quickly in a daisy mould.

The dot imprint mat enables perfect placement of the pearls on the bottom tier. The top tier must be marked for placement by hand to match the tier under it.

The decorative sugar pearls can be made in advance and stored, but the rope must be positioned around the cake while still soft.

An additional 46cm (18in) green florist's foil covered board was added for a colour accent under the cake for final presentation.

19cm (7½in) card or board directly under the cake. Coat with buttercream.

4 Ice both cakes with buttercream. Allow the icing to dry to the touch and use an unpatterned paper towel and sugarpaste smoother to continue the smoothing.

5 Imprint the 30cm (12in) tier with the 2cm (¾in) dot mat around the sides of the base cake.

6 Apply the puppy stencil steps on the slanted top cake, following the directions on page 158.

7 Using the strip cutter, cut strips from the lime sugarpaste (see page 159). Dampen the back of each with a paintbrush and water, then line up the stripes of sugarpaste with every fourth vertical line of dots on the larger tier up and over the top and to the base of the 20cm (8in) cake.

8 Match the base-tier dot pattern and add the lines up the sides of the slanted top tier.

9 Soften the 450g (1lb) sugarpaste (rolled fondant) with piping gel and divide into three portions; colour one third yellow and one third green. Lay the three long rolls of coloured sugarpaste side by side and roll into one larger roll. Place in the cookie press with the larger rope disc, with one colour showing in each clover leaf section. Extract a long strip and twist making the multi-coloured sugarpaste rope to go around the base of the cake. Trim at an angle following the rope pattern and match the two ends to give a seamless rope border. The cookie press will hold enough sugarpaste to make a base-border for a 38cm (15in), 28cm (11in) and 18cm (7in) three-tier cake. (The clover leaf disc can be ordered from Earlene's Cakes, see list of suppliers on page 198–199).

10 Add dots of buttercream and a 5mm (⅕in) sugarpaste pearl on each of the dots on the bottom tier. Add 4mm (⅙in) dots and pearls on the top tier following the same pattern as the base tier, only slightly closer together.

11 Add the flower paste (gum paste) daisies and leaves and moulded daisies for the final touches to the cake.

Chocolate groom's cake

This mouthwatering chocolate cake is accented with chocolate-dipped strawberries. Edible copper nails, a buttercream-stencilled initial and simple textures give this design simple elegance in chocolate tones.

---

1 Make 400 sugarpaste (rolled fondant) nail heads. Dry overnight, then paint the tops with a mixture of copper dusting powder and lemon extract (see page 159).
2 Ice each cake with chocolate cream cheese buttercream icing. Smooth with unpatterned paper towels or a piece of fine gauze and a sugarpaste smoother.

ASSEMBLING THE CAKE

3 Assemble the cake from the bottom as follows: puff base, 35cm (14in) white (crystal leg set) plate, 34cm (13¹/2in) round cake card covered on one side with contact paper, two-layer

Use diamond and line imprint mats for simple yet effective side patterns on the cakes. Press the mat into the icing to create the pattern.

Cake and Decoration

- 400 sugarpaste (rolled fondant) nail heads (see page 159)
- 35cm (14in) round, 23cm (9in) square and 20cm (8in) round cakes
- 2.75kg (6lb) chocolate cream cheese buttercream icing (see page 187)
- 56cm (22in) puff base (EM)
- 35cm (14in) white (crystal leg set) plate (W)
- 33.5cm (13¹/2in) round, 21.5cm (8¹/2in) square, 19cm (7¹/2in) round cake cards
- chocolate brown and green food colourings
- brown/green airbrush food colourings
- fresh strawberries
- 250g (8oz) each of white, milk and dark chocolate (summer coating)
- 50g (2oz) chocolate sugarpaste (rolled fondant)
- decorative leaves

Special Equipment

- sugarpaste smoother
- diamond and line mats (EM)
- contact paper
- 20cm (8in) and 15cm (6in) stress-free support rings with legs
- 2 mylar, wax or transparency sheets
- templates (see page 197)
- small angled spatulas
- nos. 2, 3, 18 and 20 piping tubes (tips)
- airbrush

The Old English/Gothic letter must be applied to the top of the slanted tier before any other decorating can be completed on the top surface.

Long slender areas should be filled from the ends towards the centre, to prevent pushing icing under the edges of the patterns and distorting the design.

To accentuate the outline, pipe with a darker shade of chocolate icing. Check out your computer fonts to find lettering styles.

35cm (14in) round cake, 20cm (8in) stress-free ring with legs, 21cm (8¹/2in) square cake cardboard covered on both sides with contact paper, two-layer 23cm (9in) square cake, 15cm (6in) stress-free support ring, 19cm (7¹/2in) round cake cardboard covered on both sides with contact paper, two-layer 20cm (8in) round cake with slanted top (see Puppy love on page 165).

DECORATING THE CAKE

4 Imprint the diamond and line mats on the cake sides. Begin and end the diamond and line imprint on each of the mats approximately 2.5cm (1in) from the edges to prevent imprinting a vertical line from the edge of the mats. Match the pattern and continue imprinting around the cake. (A buttercream icing that is dry to the touch is required for best results.)

5 Imprint the sides of the base tier with the triangle and small square shapes cut from the line mat. Imprint the middle tier and the top tier with the diamond mat. Cut and use the small diamond line pattern to imprint some of the diamonds in the middle tier to form a pattern in the centre of that tier, as shown.

STENCILLED INITIAL

6 To apply the stencilled initial to the top of the cake, first outline the outer edges of the letter from the template on sheets of mylar, wax paper or Dura-lar sheets for the first layer. Place the stencil pattern over cardboard and cut the stencil with a craft knife.

7 Add brown-green colour to the chocolate buttercream icing to make a darker brown colour. Place the stencil on the top of the dry-to-the-touch icing. Use an angled spatula to fill the cut out area from the outside edges to the centre, following the same instructions as used on the Puppy love stencils on page 158.

8 Outline the inside pattern area on the template sheet for the second layer stencil and add a few dotted lines to

guide you in placement over the first stencil. Proceed as before to cut out the pattern and, using a small angled spatula, follow the previous instructions to add a thin layer of the same icing used for the cake. Gently flatten the letter using paper towel or fine gauze and a smoother.

9 Fill a small bag with the dark buttercream icing and, using a piping bag fitted with a no. 2 piping tube (tip), outline the edges of the letter.

FINISHING TOUCHES

10 Airbrush the cake top with brown/green colour from the top cake edge, feathering out in the centre. Airbrush the centre lined pattern on the middle tier and lined sections on the base.

11 Pipe decorative lines on the middle and bottom tiers with a no. 3 tube and dark brown icing.

12 Pipe a few dots of icing and carefully attach the sugarpaste nail heads as shown in the photograph.

13 Pipe reverse shells with a piping tube fitted with a no. 18 tube at the base and top edge of each tier.

14 About 3 hours before the cake is to be served, wash the strawberries and reserve a third of the nicest berries to leave plain. Dip six of the best strawberries in white chocolate up to the caylx. When the white is set, dip at an angle into milk chocolate on each side.

15 Pipe a lapel, bow tie and buttons with dark chocolate placed in a small piping bag with a scissor-cut plain tube.

16 Dip a third of the strawberries in milk chocolate and a third in dark. Arrange on a bed of washed fresh leaves.

PROFESSIONAL TIP

• Two stencil sheets will be needed for most Old English capital letters such as 'A', 'B' and 'C'. Only the letters 'I', 'X' and 'Z' in this font require one stencil.

Airbrushing gives a professional finish to the decoration. Once mastered, it is a wonderful technique, allowing soft colour shading to accent your designs.

Pipe the decorative shell borders around the top and bottom of the cakes using a simple shell or an alternate shell design.

The waistcoat and jacket are piped on to a strawberry for the ultimate finishing detail – a festive, masculine touch to this luscious groom's cake.

Rose buttercream wedding cake

Perfect for that spring or summer wedding, this stunning cake will add a touch of elegance to the special day. Roses complement the raspberries and create a unique touch to impress all the guests.

ROSES

1 Attach a piece of wax paper to a flower nail. Using a no. 12 piping tube (tip) and stiff consistency cream or pink buttercream icing, pipe a base in the shape of a cone. With a no. 104 petal tube, using the wide end down, pipe a single petal, wrapping it around the base. Continue with the next row of three petals. Hold the tube flatter as you pipe each row of petals.

2 Finish the roses with another row of five petals. Make 80 roses. Let the roses air-dry for 48 hours.

■ If you hold the piping tube flatter as you pipe each row of rose petals, the roses will look open and more full of life.

Cake and Decoration

- 1 recipe buttercream icing for roses (see page 186): 725g (1¹/₂lb/3 cups) cream, 725g (1¹/₂lb/3 cups) pink
- ¹/₂ recipe buttercream icing for stems and leaves: 115g (4oz/¹/₂ cup) avocado green, 115g (4oz/¹/₂ cup) light avocado green
- 80 sugar roses
- 450g (1lb) claret sugarpaste (rolled fondant), see step 4
- 70 moulded raspberries
- plum dusting powder
- 35cm (14in) round cake
- 25cm (10in) round cake
- 15cm (6in) round cake
- 5 recipes white buttercream icing for cakes and borders
- 45cm (18in) round cake board
- 28cm (11in) round cake board
- 18cm (7in) round cake board
- 4 stemmed glasses
- 2.25m (90in) 1mm (¹/₂₅in) wide ribbon
- silver cake base

Special Equipment

- flower nail
- nos. 3, 4, 6, 12,104 and 352 piping tubes (tips)
- raspberry mould
- paintbrush
- 15 dowel rods
- 18cm (7in) plexiglass circle

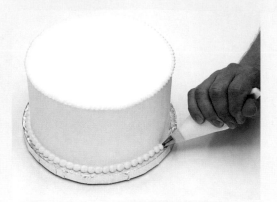

If you are piping the top and bottom borders in two different sizes, pipe the larger border on the bottom and the smaller one on the top.

Remember that when you are piping the green flower stems it is best not to pipe all the way to the edge of the cake.

A variety of sugar flowers and berries in different colours can be used to complement the theme of this cake for any occasion.

LEAVES

3 Using the no. 352 leaf tube, pipe avocado green leaves, starting with a heavy pressure, then lessening as you move outwards. For standing leaves, hold the bag at a 90-degree angle; for flatter leaves, hold the bag at a 45-degree angle as you pipe.

RASPBERRIES

4 To colour the sugarpaste (rolled fondant), use claret colour with a little light pink added. Mould the sugarpaste into the raspberry moulds by pressing firmly to ensure that all the details of the mould are achieved. Press gently to release from the mould and leave to dry. Once the raspberries are air-dried, dust them lightly with plum dusting powder.

COVERING THE CAKES

5 Smoothly ice the three cakes with the white buttercream icing. Position on the cake boards.
6 With a no. 4 piping tube and medium-consistency buttercream icing, hold the bag at a 45-degree angle and pipe a bead border on the top edge of the smallest cake. Using a no. 6 tube, pipe the same border around the base of the cake.

CAKE TOP DECORATION

7 Using a no. 3 piping tube and thin-consistency green buttercream icing, pipe the stems on the cake, holding the bag at a 45-degree angle. Pipe the stems with a flowing movement, finishing the ends with a curl.
8 Once the main stems have been piped, pipe the secondary stems connecting to the main stem and flowing out from it.
9 Using the same colour icing, pipe a mound of icing in the centre of the stems. This will give your roses some height and depth. Using the air-dried roses, pipe a medium-sized dot of icing on the bottom of each rose to

attach them. Arrange the roses by working from the centre outwards.

10 When all the roses have been arranged on the cake, position the raspberries as fillers, filling in the gaps and the outer edges of the floral spray. To finish arranging the floral spray, use a no. 352 leaf tube and medium-consistency buttercream to pipe the leaves. Using the different shades of avocado green icing, pipe the leaves, filling in between the roses and berries as needed.

ASSEMBLY

11 To stack the iced cakes, first measure the dowel rods, then cut and place them in the centres of the middle and bottom cakes for support. When the cakes have been dowelled, gently place the middle cake on top of the bottom cake, making sure it is evenly centred.

12 Ice the top of the plexiglass circle smoothly in white buttercream. Position the iced circle in the centre top of the middle cake and pipe a bead border around the edge using a no. 3 piping tube and white buttercream. Pipe all the remaining borders on all the edges of the cakes, as explained in step 6. Ice the top of the plexiglass circle smoothly in white buttercream. You can use an un-iced mirror the same size in place of the plexiglass for a different effect.

13 Take the stemmed glasses and position them evenly in quarters on top of the icing-covered plexiglass circle. When doing this, be sure to leave room for the floral spray. When the glasses are removed, the circle indentations will remain in the icing. Use these as your guides when arranging the floral spray.

14 Arrange the floral spray borders around the bottom edges of the two stacked cakes using the techniques explained above. Trim the cake boards with the ribbon.

15 Finally, position the glasses back in place where previously marked and carefully place the top cake on the glasses. Place the cake on the silver cake base.

■ The leaves may be piped with a variety of different leaf piping tubes, such as nos. 67, 352 and 74, depending on the style of leaf you want to achieve.

■ The roses and leaves can be piped or moulded in any decorating medium, such as royal icing, buttercream, sugarpaste, rolled buttercream or marzipan.

■ Any style or colour of stemmed glasses could be used to follow through a specific colour theme throughout the cake.

175

Heart in rolled buttercream

With its soft pastel shades, this beautiful elegant cake would make a perfect centrepiece for Valentine's Day, Mother's Day, a bridal shower or a birthday cake for that special someone.

COVERING THE CAKE

1 To prepare the cake, cover it in the rolled buttercream icing, rolling out the icing between the sheets of plastic (see page 157). Cover the cake board in decorative pink foil. Place the cake on the heart-shaped board.

APPLE BLOSSOM

2 For each apple blossom, attach a piece of wax paper to the flower nail. With a piping bag fitted with a no. 101 piping tube (tip) and pink royal icing, pipe the first petal, holding the tube

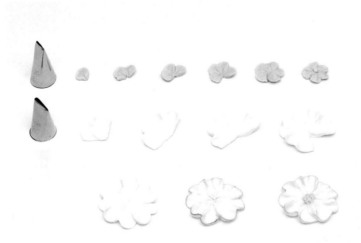

■ The apple blossom and primrose decorative piped flowers can be made in advance and stored until required.

Cake and Decoration

- 23cm (9in) heart-shaped cake
- 1 recipe rolled buttercream icing (see page 187)
- 28cm (11in) heart-shaped covered board
- decorative pink foil
- $4^1/2$ cups royal icing (see page 186): 1 cup pink, $1/4$ cup yellow, 3 cups white
- pink dusting powder
- $1/2$ recipe buttercream icing (see page 186): $1/4$ cup avocado green, $1/4$ cup light avocado green, 2 cups white, $1/4$ cup pink

Special Equipment

- 2 sheets 50cm (20in) square upholstery plastic
- 25 x 2.5cm (1in) wax paper squares
- flower nail
- 10 piping bags
- nos. 2, 3, 6, 101, 104, 352 and (PME) 43 piping tubes (tips)
- flower formers
- paintbrush

When piping the main green heart stem, it is always best to impress a pattern into the rolled buttercream as a guide.

The secondary flower stems, made up of a series of dots, should curve and flow to give the floral spray a natural effect.

When attaching the flowers to the arrangement, use the same shade of green as for the stems, so that the icing will not be noticeable.

on its side. The wide end should be in the centre of the flower and the thin end out on the edge of the flower nail.

3 Continue to pipe the remaining four petals using the same technique. Place the apple blossom on a curved flower former to dry.

4 Once the flower is dry, pipe a yellow royal icing centre using a no. 2 piping tube. Pipe a dot in the centre, continuing with four more dots surrounding the first but not touching each other.

PRIMROSES

5 For each primrose, attach a piece of wax paper to the flower nail. Using white royal icing and a no. 104 piping tube, pipe the first petal holding the tube on its side. The wide end should be in the centre of the flower nail and the thin end on the outer edge of the flower nail. When piping the petals, move the tube out 6mm (1/4in), then back inwards. This will make a heart-shaped petal.

6 Pipe the remaining four petals using the same technique. Place on a flower former to dry.

7 Once the primroses are completely dry, dust the edges slightly using pink dusting powder.

8 Pipe the centres using yellow royal icing and a no. 2 piping tube. Pipe a dot in the centre of the flower, continuing with a series of several dots surrounding the first dot and touching each other.

FLOWER STEM DESIGN

9 Using a thin-consistency green buttercream icing and no. 2 piping tube, pipe the primary heart-shaped vine.

10 Once the primary stem has been piped, pipe the secondary stems. Using a no. 2 piping tube and green buttercream icing, pipe a curved line consisting of a series of dots curving upwards towards the top of the heart-shaped stem. Start at each side of the bottom point of the heart, working your way upwards as you pipe.

11 Arrange the flowers on the stems, starting with the primroses. Pipe a dot of royal icing on the back of each flower, then attach it to the main stem.

12 Once the primroses have been placed in position, attach the apple blossoms using the same technique described, filling in where needed.

LEAVES

13 Using a no. 352 piping tube and both shades of green medium-consistency buttercream icing, pipe leaves in various sizes and shades; this will depend on the amount of pressure you apply when piping. When piping the leaves, tuck the tube under the edge of the flower and pipe outwards, filling in as needed.

FINISHING TOUCHES

14 Along the bottom edge of the cake, pipe a bead border using a piping bag fitted with a no. 43 piping tube and white royal icing to match the cake covering.

15 To accent the bead border, simply pipe small hearts using pink buttercream icing and a no. 3 piping tube to complete the cake.

PROFESSIONAL TIPS

• To stiffen rolled buttercream for modelling, knead in 50g (2oz/^{1}/2 cup) icing (confectioner's) sugar for every 225g (8oz/1 cup) rolled buttercream.

• If rolled buttercream rips while applying, it can be smoothed out by using a metal spatula and medium pressure.

Tuck the apple blossoms under the primroses for a more attractive, natural effect. Make a few extra flowers to surround the cake board.

The two different shades of avocado green icing can be used to pipe the decorative leaves, to add variety and dimension.

To finish, pipe a bead border in white royal icing and pink hearts. The colours of these flowers can be varied to coordinate with the colour theme of the occasion.

Gingerbread house

This sumptuous gingerbread house will appeal to chocolate lovers and children especially. It will make a perfect centrepiece on Thanksgiving and Christmas buffet tables or for any special occasion.

PREPARING THE GINGERBREAD

1 Cut out the templates to the dimensions required. You will need front and back pieces (the front will have the doorway and windows cut out), two side walls, identical in size, and two roof pieces, identical in size.

2 Roll out the gingerbread dough to a thickness of 6mm (1/4in) on parchment paper. Lay the house pattern on top of the rolled-out dough and, using a pizza cutter or similar, cut around the pattern. Lift the template away and remove excess dough for later use.

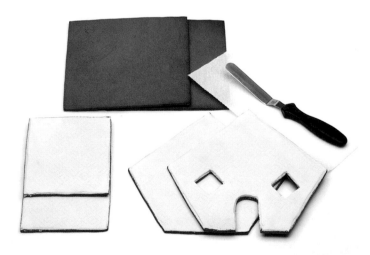

When rolling out gingerbread pieces, make the roof pieces slightly thinner: if they are a lighter weight, they are less likely to slide off during construction.

House and Decoration

- 1 recipe gingerbread (see page 187)
- 2 recipes royal icing (see page 186)
- brown food colouring
- 1 sheet gelatine
- picture frame/covered board
- 1.5kg (3lb) dark chocolate or chocolate candy coating
- 150 coconut cookies
- 7 chocolate malted balls
- 8 filled cookie logs
- 20 chocolate-covered raisins
- 40 caramels
- 36 pretzel sticks
- 24–30 chocolate truffles/chocolate balls
- chocolate-painted ice cream cone
- 30 praline chocolate discs
- 18 jelly beans
- 4 coconut macaroons

Special Equipment

- templates (see page 197)
- pizza cutter or similar
- parchment paper
- textured paper towels
- nos. 2, 3, 14, 16, 18, and 233 piping tubes (tips)
- spatulas

When positioning the second wall, it is best to prop the back wall up with a glass, jar or something similar until the icing is dry.

When positioning the gingerbread house on the board, consider the angle to give the house some character and appeal.

You might want to add charming interior details to the house. When anyone peaks through the windows, they will be delighted.

3 Using the excess gingerbread dough, roll out and cut out the four shutters and one door. Also cut out 40 odd shaped rectangles/triangles for the roof trim and two gingerbread men.

4 Bake the gingerbread pieces on baking trays in a preheated oven at 180°C/350°F (gas mark 4) for 12–15 minutes until lightly golden brown in colour. (Keep in mind that larger pieces will require longer baking time than smaller pieces such as doors and shutters.) Remove from the oven and leave to cool on a flat surface.

5 Colour one-third of the royal icing light brown, one-third dark brown, and leave the remainder white. Using a medium-consistency white royal icing, ice the front, back and side wall pieces. Once the pieces are iced, leave them to set for about 6 minutes until the icing starts to crust over slightly.

6 With a textured paper towel, gently rub with the palm of your hand against the icing to imprint the pattern on the icing. Leave to dry for 6–12 hours.

7 Place pieces of gelatine on the backs of all the windows by attaching them with royal icing to the inside walls of the house.

CONSTRUCTING THE HOUSE

8 Using a picture frame and covered cake board, position the gingerbread house. To construct the house, start with the back wall and pipe a line of royal icing along the bottom edge and the edge that will butt up to the back wall. Pipe a line of royal icing along the bottom edge of a side wall and the edge that will butt against the back wall. Repeat this procedure for the opposite side wall.

9 Attach the front wall of the house by piping a line of royal icing along the front edges of the two side walls and also along the bottom edge of the front wall.

10 Pipe a line of icing along the top edge of the walls. Attach one side of the roof and then the other side.

DECORATING THE HOUSE

11 Once the house has dried for about 24 hours, the decorating can begin. Starting with the roof, attach the cookies using a dot of royal icing on the backs. Always start from the bottom edge of the roof and work upwards to create a layering effect.

12 When both sides are complete, pipe a zig-zag border in light brown icing along the top roof edges. Press chocolate malted balls into this border.

13 Trim all the small rectangle/triangle pieces for the roof trim. With a no. 2 tube (tip), outline each with a small bead border in light brown icing.

14 Pipe a small zig-zag border along the seams of the side wall corners and across the front of the house. Attach the cookie logs.

15 Pipe a zig-zag border along the front edge of the roof and attach the rectangles/triangles before the icing sets. Pipe a zig-zag border along the bottom edges of the roof and along the back edges of the roof. Attach the rectangle/triangle pieces before the icing sets.

16 Using dark brown royal icing, pipe a Swiss dot flower embroidery design on the top section of the front and back walls of the house.

Another option before the roof is positioned is to add a little gift for each guest. When the house is taken apart, everyone will receive a present.

Pipe a line of icing along the top of the first roof piece, then add the second roof, making sure both sides are angled equally.

When making your selection of cookies, candies or other confectionery to decorate the roof, keep in mind that lighter, less bulky items are recommended.

PROFESSIONAL TIPS

• Cover your patterns with clear contact paper, to preserve them for years to come.

• Be sure to use a thick sturdy board under your house.

• Try to avoid using boiled sweets or candies when decorating your house, as they tend to melt in humidity.

• Always try to keep your house as edible as possible. Shy away from using plastic decorations.

When most of the decorating has been finished, pipe tiny flowers on the top section of the house at the front and back.

To add your personal touch, consider making a curved pathway and possibly uniquely shaped doors, windows and shutters.

When deciding on how to decorate your house, visit supermarkets and stores to check out the latest range of candies and confectionery available.

17 Trim the windows with a small shell border using a no. 14 tube, then attach the shutters.

18 Pipe embroidery and a handle on the front door. Continue by piping a trim on the edge of the door and archway door trim, using a no. 3 tube. Before the icing begins to set, attach the door to the house, opened slightly to invite 'guests'.

PATHWAY

19 Using white royal icing or white chocolate, spread a pathway on the board from the front door outwards. Before the icing sets, press chocolate-covered raisins into the pathway as stepping stones.

FINISHING TOUCHES

20 To make the trees, attach a series of truffles, starting with a larger amount at the base and working upwards in a pyramid shape; use melted chocolate to attach them together. For a different tree, use a painted ice cream cone and attach chocolate discs, working again from the bottom upwards.

21 Melt the dark chocolate to a spreadable consistency, then spread over the board to represent a yard area, remembering not to bring it to the edges of the board. Before the chocolate begins to set, position and place the chocolate trees, gingerbread men, plain or piped macaroons, candies, etc.

22 Using a piping bag fitted with a no. 233 tube and dark brown icing, pipe sprigs of grass-like patches.

FENCE

23 To build the fence, stack two caramels on top of each other using brown royal icing. Criss-cross two pretzel sticks between the caramel posts, then pipe a brown royal icing rosette to cover the top of the posts and pretzel sticks. Place a jellybean, candy or sweet of your choice on top of the rosette.

Basic recipes

SUGARPASTE (ROLLED FONDANT)

Sugarpaste (rolled fondant) is an easy-to-use icing that is pliable yet not sticky. It is ideal for covering cakes, producing a smooth, satin finish, and can be shaped into all kinds of cake decorations as shown throughout the book.

- 60g (2oz/¼ cup) white vegetable fat (shortening)
- 30ml (2 tablespoons) lemon juice
- 30ml (2 tablespoons) water
- 750g (1½lb/6 cups) icing (confectioner's) sugar, sifted

1 Put the vegetable fat, lemon juice and water into a medium-sized pan. Heat gently, stirring occasionally until the fat has melted. Stir in 225g (8oz/2 cups) of the sugar and keep stirring until the sugar has dissolved. Leave the pan over a low heat until the mixture boils, paying careful attention. Remove the pan from the heat.

2 Gradually add enough of the remaining sugar to form a soft paste, beating well after each addition. Beat the icing until smooth.

3 Lightly dust a work surface with icing (confectioner's) sugar, then knead the icing continually until smooth, silky and no longer sticky, kneading in more sugar if necessary.

4 Tint with food colouring if desired, then use immediately or store in a plastic bag. This paste keeps well in the freezer.

FLOWER PASTE (GUM PASTE)

This paste is for making sugar flowers and requires the use of a heavy-duty mixer to produce it. This flower paste uses gum tragacanth instead of tylose (CMC).

- 450g (1lb/4 cups) icing (confectioner's) sugar, sifted
- 15ml (3 teaspoons) gum tragacanth
- 25ml (5 teaspoons) cold water
- 10ml (2 teaspoons) powdered gelatine
- 15ml (3 teaspoons) white vegetable fat (shortening)
- 10ml (2 teaspoons) liquid glucose
- 35ml (7 teaspoons) reconstituted dried albumen

1 Sift the icing (confectioner's) sugar and gum tragacanth into an ovenproof bowl and place in a cool oven (100°C/ 210°F, gas mark ¼) for about 20 minutes. The sugar should be warm to the touch.

2 Place the water in a heatproof jug, sprinkle in the gelatine and leave to soak. Stand the jug in a pan of water over a low heat and stir until clear and thoroughly dissolved (to avoid a sandy texture later). *Do not boil.*

3 Add the vegetable fat and liquid glucose and heat gently until all the three ingredients are liquified.

4 Remove the sugar and gum from the oven and add the dissolved liquid and the albumen, blending with a wooden spoon. (At this stage, speed is important as the mixture cools very quickly.)

5 Insert the bowl into the mixer with the flat ('K') beater fitted and mix for about 5 minutes at the lowest speed. The grey slushy mixture should become white and 'stringy'. Insufficient beating will result in an off-white coloured paste which is too soft – the mixture should be gummy and stringy, but snow-white and firm to the touch. (*Do not* leave the mixer unattended while beating, since the mixture becomes very stiff; it is a good idea to press down on the mixer arm to prevent or reduce strain on the motor.)

6 Put the mixture in a clean airtight plastic bag, squeezing out any air, and leave to cool. When cold, place in an airtight container in the refrigerator for 24 hours before using. The paste will set quite firm.

7 When required, lightly grease your hands with some vegetable fat and thoroughly knead a piece the size of a golf ball until it is soft, elastic and pliable. If too dry, add a small amount of fat, or if crumbly, add some liquid albumen. Remember that fat slows down the drying process, while extra albumen makes the paste more pliable. The paste should always be stored in a refrigerator and will keep for 6–8 weeks. The paste is also suitable for freezing.

TYLOSE FLOWER PASTE (GUM PASTE)

Tylose (CMC) is an alternative product for making flower paste (gum paste) instead of gum tragacanth. The advantage of tylose is that the paste is less expensive, easier to make, holds up better in humidity and is whiter in colour.

- 4 large egg whites
- 900g (2lb) icing (confectioner's) sugar, sifted
- 60ml (12 teaspoons) tylose (CMC)
- 20ml (4 teaspoons) white vegetable fat (shortening)

1 Place the egg whites in a heavy-duty mixer bowl, fitted with the flat paddle. Turn the mixer on high speed for 10 seconds to break up the egg whites.

2 Reserve 115g (4oz /1 cup) of the icing (confectioner's) sugar and set aside. Turn the mixer to the lowest speed and slowly add the remaining sugar. This will make a soft-consistency royal icing.

3 Turn up the speed to setting 3 or 4 for about 2 minutes. During this time, measure the tylose into a small container.

4 Make sure the mixture is at soft-peak stage. It should look shiny, meringue-like, with the peaks falling over. When making this paste, it is possible to colour an entire batch, making it ideal if you have a lot of flowers or leaves to make in a certain colour. (If colouring the entire batch, add the food colouring at this stage, making it a shade darker than the desired colour because when the tylose and the remaining icing sugar are added, it will make the colour a little lighter.) The alternative is to make white paste, then cut off the quantity you require to make the colour desired.

5 Turn the mixer to the slow setting and sprinkle the tylose in over a 5-second time period. Next, turn the speed up to the high setting for a few seconds. (This will thicken the mixture.)

6 Scrape the mixture out of the bowl on to a work surface sprinkled with some of the reserved icing sugar. Place the white vegetable fat (shortening) on your hands and knead the paste, adding enough of the reserved sugar to form a soft but not sticky dough. Check by pinching with your fingers – they should come away clean. Place the finished paste in a zip-top bag, then place the bagged paste in a second bag and seal.

7 Place in the refrigerator for 24 hours if possible, to mature the paste before using.

8 Before use, remove from the refrigerator and allow the paste to come to room temperature. Take a small amount of vegetable fat on the end of your finger and knead into the paste. If you have made the paste white and are colouring the paste, add the food colouring at this stage.

9 Always store the paste in zip-top bags and return to the refrigerator when you are not using the paste. The paste will keep under refrigeration for about 6 months. You can keep the paste longer by freezing, using zip-top freezer bags. Allow the paste to mature for 24 hours in the refrigerator first before placing it in the freezer. Tylose flower paste can be kept in the freezer for several years with no problems.

Note: When making this paste, the amount of icing sugar that the paste will need to obtain the correct consistency will vary according to geographical location, temperature and the grading of the eggs.

ROYAL ICING

When making royal icing, the equipment must be clean, well dried and grease-free.

- 500g (1lb 2oz/4$\frac{1}{2}$ cups) icing (confectioner's) sugar, sifted
- 80g (3oz) egg white or 17g ($\frac{2}{3}$oz) egg albumen
- 80ml (2$\frac{3}{4}$fl oz/$\frac{1}{3}$ cup) water

1 Put three-quarters of the icing (confectioner's) sugar and the egg white into a mixing bowl. Beat for 2–3 minutes on slow speed with an electric mixer.

2 Beat, adding more of the icing sugar, until full-peak consistency is achieved. (When a palette knife or spoon is placed on the surface of the icing and lifted, the peak of the icing remains.)

Note: If using albumen powder, mix the powder and water in a bowl and leave for at least 2 hours, or preferably overnight.

MEXICAN PASTE

A firm paste that is ideal for cutter work.

- 225g (8oz/2 cups) icing (confectioner's) sugar
- 15ml (3 teaspoons) gum tragacanth
- 5ml (1 teaspoon) liquid glucose (optional)
- 30ml (6 teaspoons) cold water

1 Mix the icing (confectioner's) sugar and gum tragacanth in a bowl. Add the glucose, if using, and water. Knead well.

2 Place in a plastic bag at room temperature for 12 hours.

3 This paste will feel hard. To soften, break a small piece away and work until stretchy. Freeze unused paste.

BUTTERCREAM ICING

- 450g (1lb/2 cups) white vegetable fat (shortening)
- 900g (2lb/8 cups) icing (confectioner's) sugar
- 120ml (8 tablespoons) water or milk
- 10ml (2 teaspoons) clear vanilla flavouring
- 10ml (2 teaspoons) butter flavouring
- 2.5ml ($\frac{1}{2}$ teaspoon) salt

1 Combine all the ingredients in a mixing bowl in the order listed. Mix until well blended for about 7–10 minutes; the icing should be light and fluffy.

2 Refrigerate the icing when not being used. Bring to room temperature to work with. Keep the icing covered when not in use to avoid crusting over.

CREAM CHEESE BUTTERCREAM ICING

A delicious cake covering that can be flavoured in many ways.

- 900g (2lb/8 cups) icing (confectioner's) sugar
- 75ml (5 tablespoons/$^1/_3$ cup) warm water
- 7.5ml ($1^1/_2$ teaspoons) butavan (optional)
- 100g ($3^1/_2$oz) warm cream cheese
- 200g (7oz/$^7/_8$ cup) crisco (white flora/trex)

1 Mix all the ingredients together until slightly moistened.
2 Place in an electric mixer and beat at medium speed until well blended. Scrape the bowl down occasionally until all the dry ingredients are mixed in.

Chocolate: add 75g (3oz/$^3/_4$ cup) sifted cocoa powder and additional water if necessary.

Orange or lemon: add 5ml (1 teaspoon) orange or lemon emulsion.

Strawberry: add 2.5ml ($^1/_2$ teaspoon) powdered strawberry natural flavouring.

Note: Butavan is a thick flavouring emulsion that smells and looks like butterscotch. Use vanilla extract instead if necessary.

ROLLED BUTTERCREAM

- 225g (8oz/1 cup) crisco (white flora/trex)
- 225g (8oz) corn syrup
- 2.5ml ($^1/_2$ teaspoon) salt
- 1.25ml ($^1/_4$ teaspoon) lemon oil
- 1.25ml ($^1/_4$ teaspoon) orange oil
- 900g (2lb/8 cups) icing (confectioner's) sugar

1 With a heavy-duty mixer, measure all the ingredients in a mixing bowl as listed. Beat until all the ingredients are almost mixed together.
2 Turn out on a work surface and knead for 2–3 minutes until all the ingredients are thoroughly combined. The mixture should not feel sticky at all. If it does, add more icing sugar, a small amount at a time, until it is not sticky. It keeps well in the refrigerator. Bring to room temperature before using.

EDIBLE GLUE

Edible glue is used to secure paste together, such as making bows or attaching pieces directly to a sugarpaste (rolled fondant) surface. It can also be used in the making of sugar flowers as an alternative to egg white.

Bring 250ml (8fl oz /1 cup) water to a rolling boil in a small pan and remove from heat. Add 7ml (1 heaped teaspoon) tylose (CMC) powder to the water. This will go a little lumpy. Stir well with a fork to break up the tylose. Usually it takes about 30 minutes of stirring frequently for the tylose to dissolve. Allow to cool. Place in an airtight bottle when cool. Keep in the refrigerator when not in use.

PIPING GOLD AND SILVER

This makes a metallic piping medium that can be used for writing directly on to a cake surface in silver or gold or other metallic finish. It can be used for embroidery, cornelli lace, etc.

- 10ml (2 teaspoons) icing (confectioner's) sugar
- 10ml (2 teaspoons) gold, silver or metallic dusting powder
- clear alcohol (gin or vodka)
- about 5ml (1 teaspoon) piping gel

1 On a small ceramic plate, mix the sugar and gold, silver or metallic dust. Add a few drops of clear alcohol (gin or vodka) and mix with a small palette knife to create a stiff paste.
2 Add the piping gel, a little at a time, mixing well until the consistency for piping is reached. Use a very small piping bag and a no. 1 piping tube (tip) or smaller size, if needed. The mixture you have left can be put into a small container and stored in the refrigerator. It will keep indefinitely.

GINGERBREAD

- 225g (8oz/1 cup) crisco (white flora/trex)
- 225g (8oz/1 cup) white granulated sugar
- 225g (8oz) molasses
- 2 eggs, beaten
- 575g ($1^1/_4$lb/5 cups) plain (all-purpose) white flour
- 5ml (1 teaspoon) salt
- 5ml (1 teaspoon) ground cloves
- 5ml (1 teaspoon) ground nutmeg
- 10ml (2 teaspoons) ground cinnamon
- 10ml (2 teaspoons) ground ginger

1 In a microwave, heat the white fat in a mixing bowl until just melted, not hot.
2 Combine the sugar, molasses, eggs and white fat, mixing thoroughly.
3 Add the flour, salt and spices, then blend for an additional 2–3 minutes until well mixed, scraping the sides of the bowl occasionally. If the dough is not mixed completely, turn the dough on to the work surface and finish by hand kneading.

Templates

Bow (page 53)

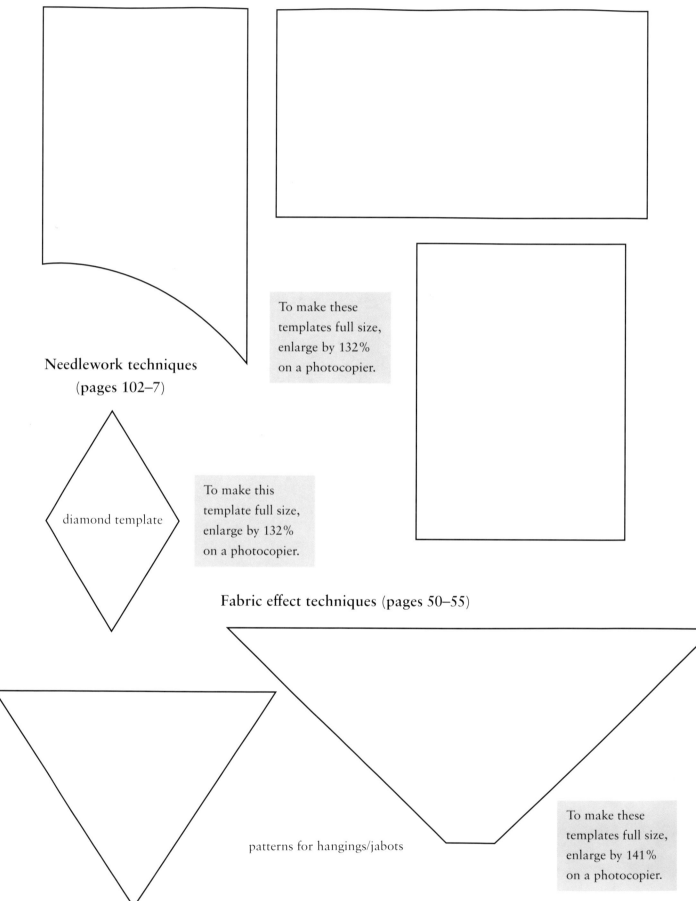

Needlework techniques
(pages 102–7)

diamond template

To make these
templates full size,
enlarge by 132%
on a photocopier.

To make this
template full size,
enlarge by 132%
on a photocopier.

Fabric effect techniques (pages 50–55)

patterns for hangings/jabots

To make these
templates full size,
enlarge by 141%
on a photocopier.

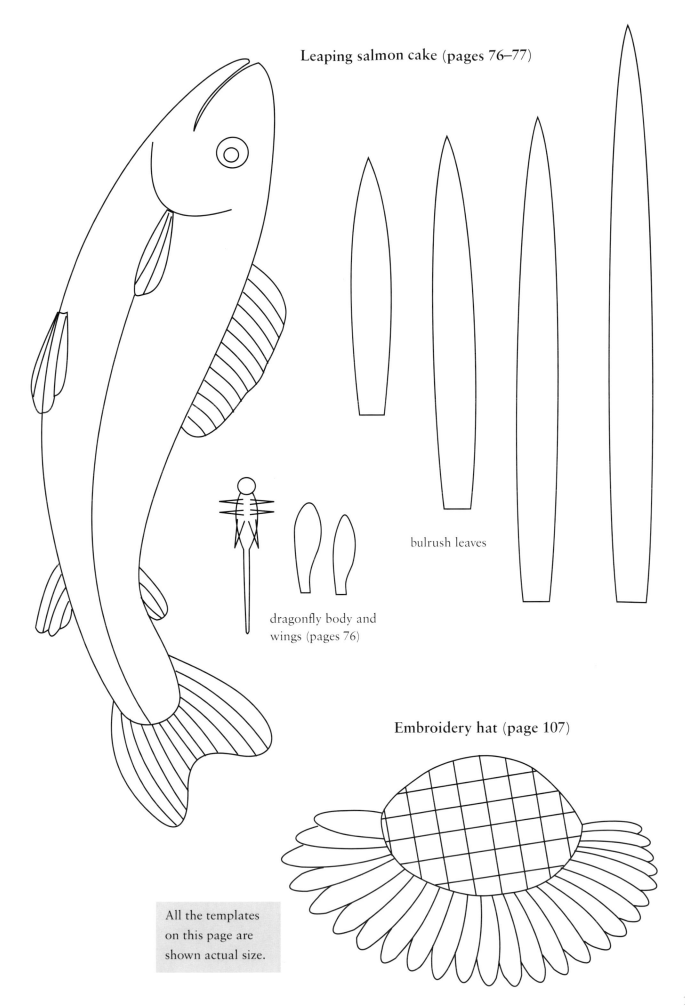

Leaping salmon cake (pages 76–77)

bulrush leaves

dragonfly body and
wings (pages 76)

Embroidery hat (page 107)

All the templates
on this page are
shown actual size.

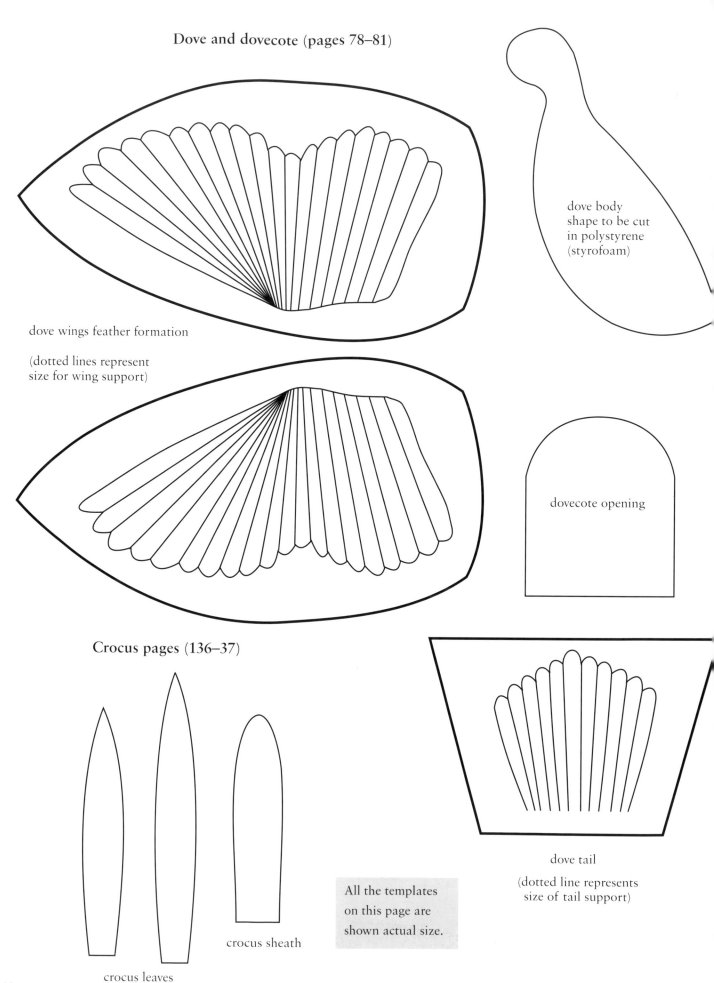

Dove and dovecote (pages 78–81)

dove body
shape to be cut
in polystyrene
(styrofoam)

dove wings feather formation

(dotted lines represent
size for wing support)

dovecote opening

Crocus pages (136–37)

dove tail

(dotted line represents
size of tail support)

All the templates
on this page are
shown actual size.

crocus sheath

crocus leaves

190

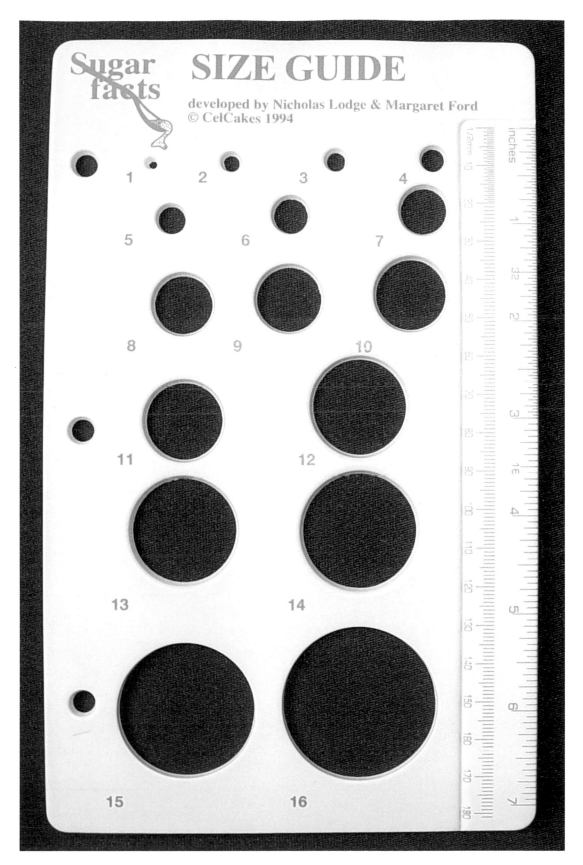

Size guide

Use this chart as reference (shown actual size).

A plastic size guide is available for purchase if desired.

Cross stitch plaque (page 105)

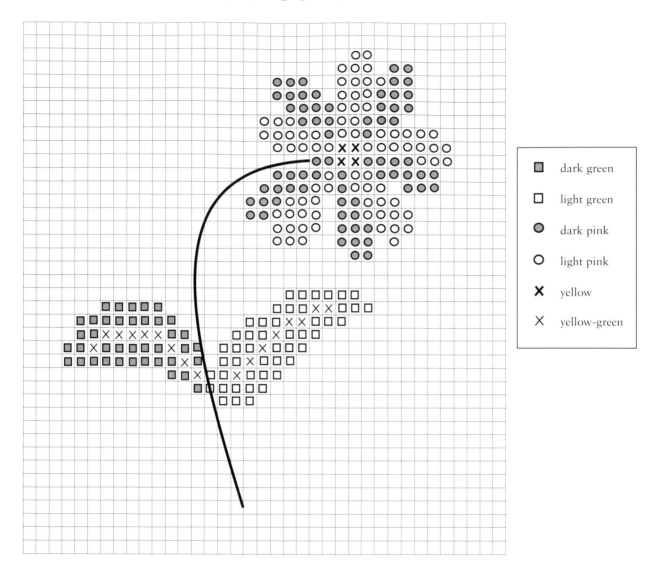

■	dark green
□	light green
●	dark pink
○	light pink
✗	yellow
✗	yellow-green

Christening babe (pages 92–94)

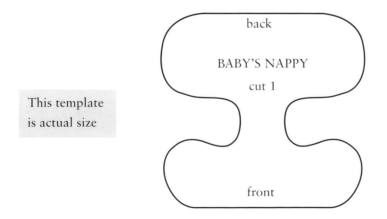

This template
is actual size

back

BABY'S NAPPY

cut 1

front

Country wedding cake (pages 88–91)

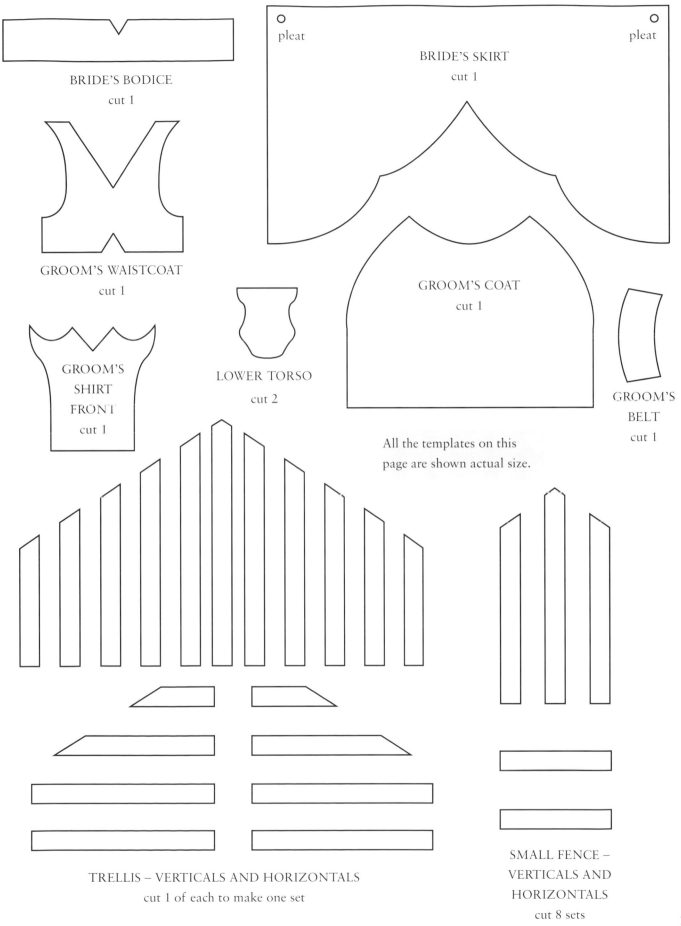

BRIDE'S BODICE
cut 1

pleat   pleat
BRIDE'S SKIRT
cut 1

GROOM'S WAISTCOAT
cut 1

GROOM'S COAT
cut 1

LOWER TORSO
cut 2

GROOM'S
SHIRT
FRONT
cut 1

GROOM'S
BELT
cut 1

All the templates on this
page are shown actual size.

TRELLIS – VERTICALS AND HORIZONTALS
cut 1 of each to make one set

SMALL FENCE –
VERTICALS AND
HORIZONTALS
cut 8 sets

Clowning around (pages 95–99)

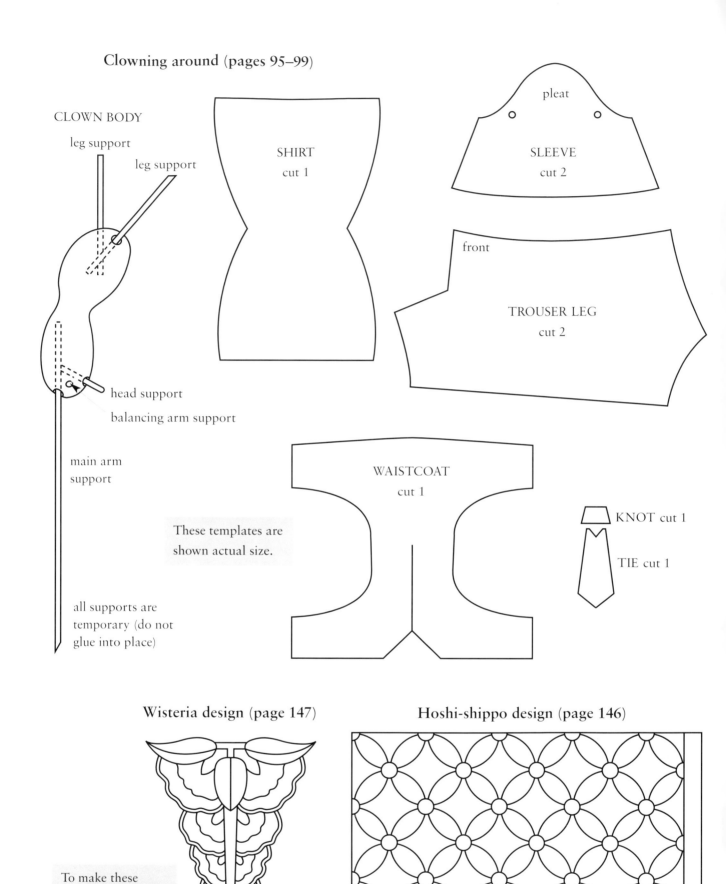

CLOWN BODY

leg support

leg support

SHIRT
cut 1

pleat

SLEEVE
cut 2

front

TROUSER LEG
cut 2

head support

balancing arm support

main arm
support

These templates are
shown actual size.

WAISTCOAT
cut 1

KNOT cut 1

TIE cut 1

all supports are
temporary (do not
glue into place)

Wisteria design (page 147)

Hoshi-shippo design (page 146)

To make these
templates full size,
enlarge by 133%
on a photocopier.

Lattice design (page 145)

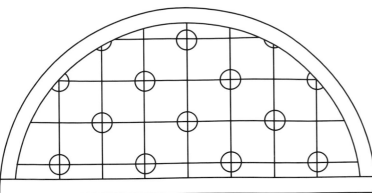

To make these templates full size, enlarge by 130% on a photocopier.

Bamboo design (page 144)

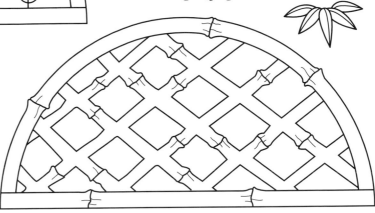

Hydrangea wedding cake (pages 152–55)

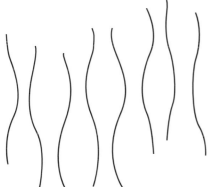

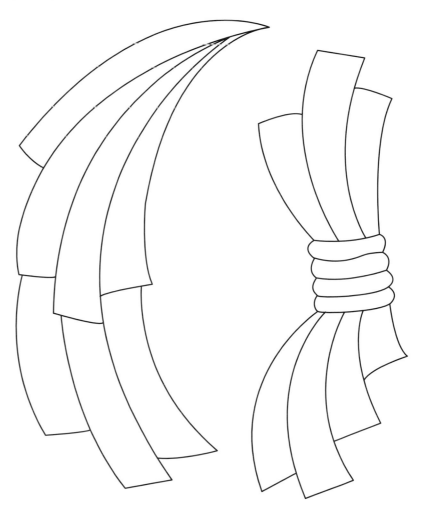

To make these templates full size, enlarge by 130% on a photocopier.

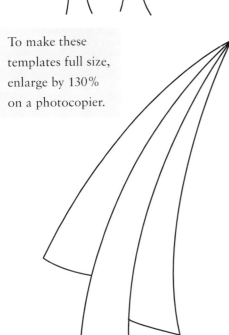

Cherry blossom celebration cake (pages 148–51)

To make these templates full size, enlarge by 131% on a photocopier.

Puppy love (pages 165–67)

pattern 2 (yellow)

pattern 1 (white)

pattern 3 (red)

pattern 6 (green)

pattern 4 (brown)

pattern 5 (black)

To make these templates full size, enlarge by 137% on a photocopier.

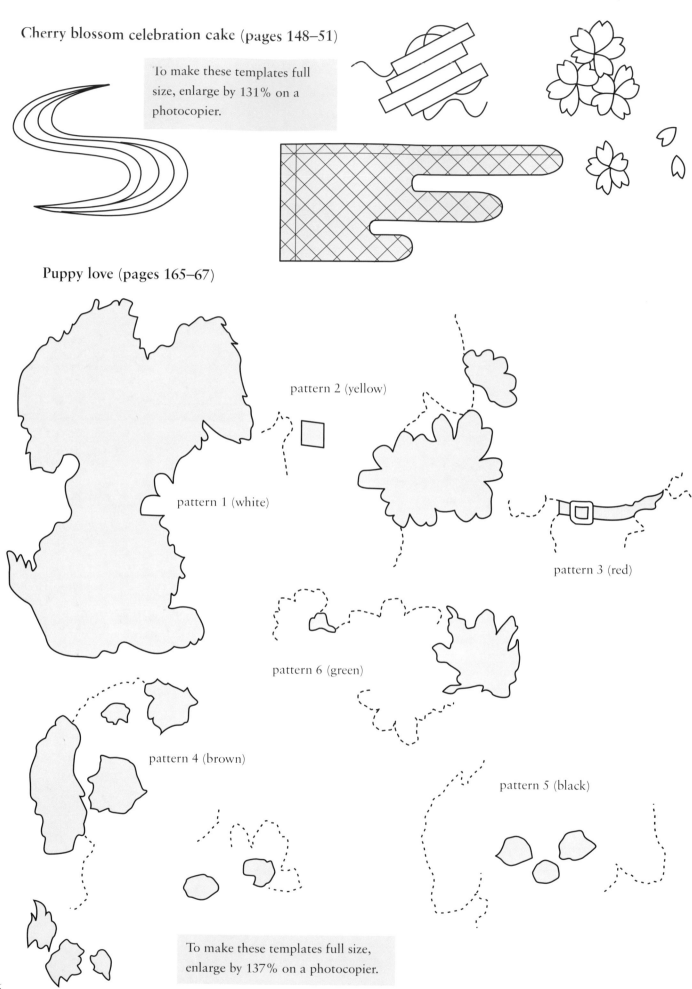

Chocolate groom's cake (pages 168–71)

R pattern 1

To make these templates full size, enlarge by 141% on a photocopier.

R pattern 2

Cut out the shaded areas for the two R stencils

Gingerbread house (pages 180–84)

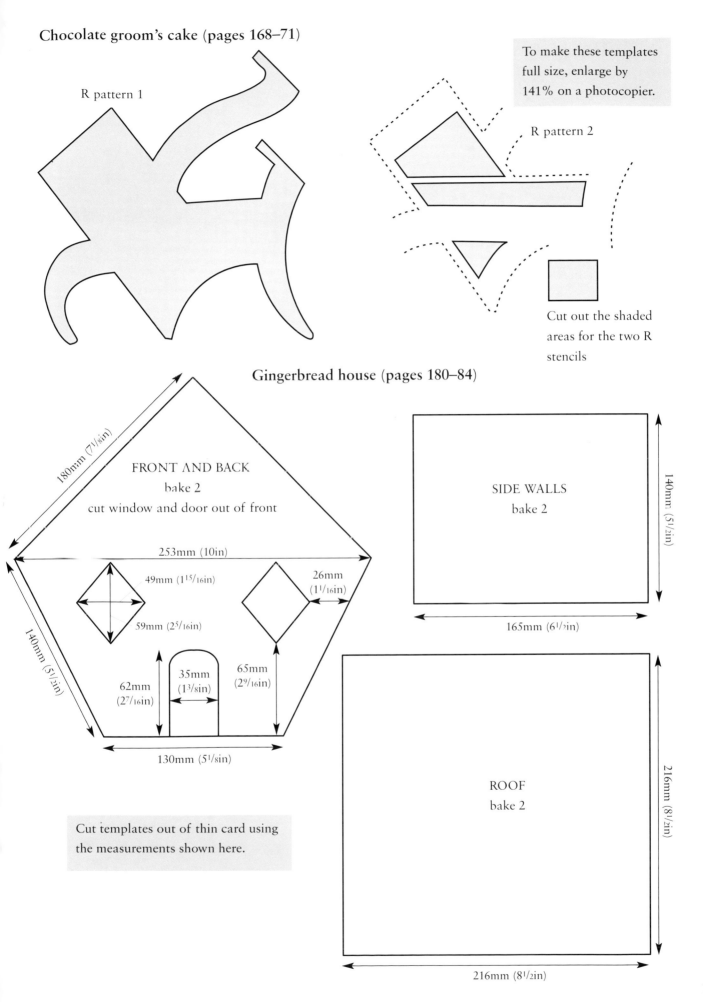

FRONT AND BACK
bake 2
cut window and door out of front

180mm (7¹/₈in)

253mm (10in)

49mm (1¹⁵/₁₆in)

26mm (1¹/₁₆in)

59mm (2⁵/₁₆in)

140mm (5¹/₂in)

62mm (2⁷/₁₆in)

35mm (1³/₈in)

65mm (2⁹/₁₆in)

130mm (5¹/₈in)

SIDE WALLS
bake 2

140mm (5¹/₂in)

165mm (6¹/₂in)

ROOF
bake 2

216mm (8¹/₂in)

216mm (8¹/₂in)

Cut templates out of thin card using the measurements shown here.

197

Suppliers and acknowledgments

Many special products and equipment have been used and shown in this book. Your local sugarcraft store should carry most of the basic equipment and some of the special equipment shown. In addition, we have listed the specialist suppliers of these products. Where applicable, in each project, a letter code has been added to refer the reader to the supplier or manufacturer of the product listed.

International Sugar Art Collection (ISAC) and CelCrafts (C) both have a mail order and internet shopping service for those readers who do not have a local retail outlet.

Nicholas Lodge
International Sugar Art Collection (ISAC)
6060 McDonough Drive
Suite F
Norcross, GA 30093-1230
USA
toll free 800-662-8925
telephone 770-453-9449
fax 770-448-9046
email: info@nicholaslodge.com
www.nicholaslodge.com

Margaret Ford
CelCakes (C)
CelCrafts and CelCakes
Springfield House
Gate Helmsley
York YO41 1NF
UK
telephone 01759 371 447
fax 01759 372513

email: info@celcrafts.co.uk
www.celcrafts.co.uk

GUEST AUTHORS CONTACT INFORMATION

Earlene Moore
Earlene's Cakes (EM)
1323 East 78th Street
Lubbock, TX 79404-6757
USA
telephone 806-745-2230
email:
earlenem@earlenescakes.com
www.earlenescakes.com

June Twelves
Holly Products (HP)
Holly Cottage
Hassall Green
Sandbach
Cheshire CW11 4YA
UK
telephone/fax 01270 761 403
email: June.Twelves@u.genie.co.uk
www.HollyProducts.co.uk

Steven Stellingwerf
2915 Lyme Grass Avenue
Sioux Falls, SD 57107
USA
telephone 605-367-6826

Marion Frost
Patchwork Cutters (PC)
3 Raines Close
Greasby
Wirral
Merseyside CH49 2QB
UK
telephone/fax 0151 678 5053

Toshie Harashima
#308 1-5-11 Yanaka
Taito-Ku
Tokyo
110-0001
JAPAN
fax 81-3-3358-6392
email: toshiecat@hotmail.com
URL: www.players.co.jp/-sugar

SUPPLIERS

UK
Culpitt Cake Art, Culpitt Ltd
Jubilee Industrial Estate
Ashington, Northumberland
NE63 8UQ
telephone 01670 814 545

Renshaw Scott Ltd
Crown Street
Liverpool, L87RF
telephone 0151 706 8200
Suppliers of Renshaw's Regalice sugarpaste used in this book

Squires Kitchen (SK)
Squires House
3 Waverley Lane
Farnham
Surrey GU9 8BB
telephone 01252 711 749

FMM (FMM)
Unit 5
Kings Park Ind. Estate
Primrose Hill
Kings Langley
Herts WD4 8ST
fax 01923 261 226
email:
clements@f-m-m.demon.co.uk

Sugar City (SC)
78 Battle Road
St Leonards-on-Sea
East Sussex TN37 7AG
telephone 01424 432 448
fax 01424 421 359
email: sugarcity@btinternet.com
www.sugarcity.co.uk

Sugarflair (SF)
Sugarflair Colours Ltd
Brunell Road
Manor Trading Estate
Benfleet, Essex SS7 4PS
telephone 01268 752 891
fax 01268 759 643

A Piece of Cake (APOC)
18 Upper High Street
Thame, Oxon OX9 3EX
tel/fax 0184 421 3428
email: sales@sugaricing.com
Supplier of flower paste
used in this book

Wilton UK (W)
Knightsbridge Bakeware
Centre UK Ltd
Chadwell Heath Lane
Romford, Essex RM6 4NP
telephone 0208 590 5959
fax 0208 590 7373
www.cakedecoration.co.uk

Guy Paul & Co. Ltd
Unit B4, Foundry Way
Little End Road, Eaton Socon
Cambs. PE19 3JH

USA

Sugar Bouquets (SB)
23 North Star Drive
Morristown, NJ 07960
telephone 973-538-3542
fax 973-538-4939
email: mail@sugarbouquets.com
www.sugarbouquets.com

CK Products (CK)
Fort Wayne, IN 46825
telephone 219-484-2517
fax 219-484-2510
email: mail@ckproducts.com
www.ckproducts.com

Wilton Industries (W)
2240 W. 75th Street
Woodbridge, IL 60517
toll free 800-794-5866
phone 630-963-7100
free fax 888-824-9520
fax 630-810-2256
email: info@wilton.com
www.wilton.com

Ateco (AT)
August Thomson Corporation
36 Sea Cliff Avenue
Glen Cove, NY 11542-3699
telephone 516-676-7100
fax 516-676-7108

Arlene Haase Cakes Inc.
(Stress-free support systems)
42551 299th Street
Scotland SD 57059
telephone 605-583-2393
ordering form:
www.earlenescakes.com/
stressfreeordfrm.htm

Creative Cutters US (CC)
2495 Main Street
Suite 410
Buffalo, NY 14214
telephone 716-831-0562
email:
creativecutters@cakeartistry.com
hyperlink:
http://www.creativecutters.com
www.creativecutters.com

OTHERS

Creative Cutters (CC)
561 Edward Avenue
Unit 2
Richmond Hill, Ontario
CANADA L4C 9W6
telephone 905-883-5638

JEM Cutters (JEM)
P.O. Box 115 Kloof 3640
Kwazulu, Natal
SOUTH AFRICA
telephone 031 7011431
email: maytham@iafrica.com

Rosa Viacava de Ortega (RVO)
Av. Brasil 1141 Jesus Maria
Lima 11, PERU
telephone 511 423 4210
telephone/fax 511 423 5986

Cupid's Cake Decorations
2/90 Belford Street, Broadmeadow
NSW 2292, AUSTRALIA
telephone +61 2 4962 1884

Cake Decorating School of
Australia
Shop 7, Port Phillip Arcade
232 Flinders Street
Melbourne, VIC 3000
telephone +61 3 9654 5335

Published by Murdoch Books®, a division of Murdoch Magazines Pty. Ltd

Murdoch Books® Australia
GPO Box 1203, Sydney NSW 1045
Phone: +61(0) 2 4352 7000   Fax: +61(0) 2 4352 7026

Murdoch Books UK Limited
Merehurst is an imprint of Murdoch Books UK Ltd
Ferry House, 51–57 Lacy Road,
Putney, London, SW15 1PR
Phone: +44(0) 20 8355 1480   Fax: +44(0) 20 8355 1499

Edited by Barbara Croxford
Designed by Maggie Aldred
Front cover cake by Margaret Ford and Nicholas Lodge,
photographed by Nigel Kirby (N & K Photographic Images UK)
Photography by Nigel Kirby
Michael Nelson Studio (US)
Kazutsugu Tsushima (Japan)

Chief Executive: Juliet Roberts
Publisher: Kay Scarlett

National Library of Australia Cataloguing-in-Publication Data
Ford, Margaret. The international school of sugarcraft. Book 3: New skills and techniques.
ISBN 1 74045 306 9
1. Sugar art. 2. Cake decorating. I. Lodge, Nicholas. II. Title.
641.8653

Printed by Midas Printing (Asia) Ltd. PRINTED IN CHINA